Every Friday Night

My Year of Dating

Misadventures

Doubleday New York London Toronto Sydney Auckland

Every Friday Night

Ritta McLaughlin

PUBLISHED BY DOUBLEDAY
a division of Random House, Inc.

DOUBLEDAY and the portrayal of an anchor with a dolphin are
registered trademarks of Random House, Inc.

The experiences recounted here actually occurred. However, the
identifying characteristics of the people portrayed have been changed to
protect their privacy.

Book design by Dana Leigh Treglia

Library of Congress Cataloging-in-Publication Data

McLaughlin, Ritta.
Every Friday night : my year of dating misadventures /
Ritta McLaughlin.— 1st ed.
p. cm.
1. Dating (Social customs)   2. Man-woman relationships.
3. Women—Attitudes.   I. Title.
HQ801.M343 2003
306.7—dc21   2003043516

ISBN 0-385-50380-6

PRINTED IN THE UNITED STATES OF AMERICA

August 2003

First Edition

1   3   5   7   9   10   8   6   4   2

For Jessie Mae and Plina Kay

My Grandmothers Who Taught Me

What Love Is

Acknowledgments

All praise and thanks to the Creator who guides and protects me.

People come and go but each person has made a difference in the quality of my life. Thank you only begins to say what blessings you have been to me:

To my family: your love gets me through

To the candles that burn so brightly especially during the thunderstorms:

D. Bailey, PB, Dean, S. Goetzinger, S. Hamer, M. Hart, S. Harriett, P. Harris, V. Hemingway, L. Heller, The Inces, S. Ivy, A. Jefferson, DJ, J. Lee, The Liburds, A. Matos, E. Munroe, T. Odom, Ms. Perry, G. Ruffin, A. Robinson, S. Robinson, R. Sallis, M. Seligmon, The Sheingolds, J. Soltz, The Sullivans, N. Vocy, W. Washington.

I am inspired and encouraged by the lives you live and the love you bring to the world.

To the crew in the Sag Harbor House—who let me write in peace.

Many special thanks to the talented team that has made this idea more than just a notion:

Janet Hill—my editor extraordinaire—and her assistant Tracy Jacobs: You move mountains and make the seas stand still. If only you could bottle and sell your patience and persistence.

Tanya McKinnon, my agent: You are masterful. Your never-ending enthusiasm, encouragement, and straight talk have made all the difference. I could not have done this without you.

Gordon Bobb, Esq.: Your friendship and advice keep me out of trouble. Richard Simon: For reading, re-reading, listening, and reading again—you have given me hope.

Kelli Martin: I will always be grateful for your encouraging me to share.

For those of you who I didn't mention *(you know who you are)*: I couldn't have written this book without you. (This applies to the guilty and the innocent.)

Contents

Contents

Introduction

My Grandma always said . . .
Yes, there's plenty of fish in the sea.
But sometimes you catch the big one and
have to throw him back. Sometimes you
catch nothing, and have to remember why
you're fishing in the first place. And most of
the time you've got to keep fishing
just to learn a thing or two.

The quest for Mr. Right, especially in New York City, takes fortitude, clarity, intuition, patience, divine intervention, and most important, a sense of humor. The more people I talk with, the surer I am that sooner or later the dating malaise hits everyone. Dating can make you wonder if you've been cast in a real-life sitcom, caught in a Greek tragedy, or just begun losing your mind. So if you ever thought that you're more likely to find the Holy Grail than your soul mate . . . well, you're not alone.

Every Friday Night is the story of my misadventures on the quest for Mr. Right in the year before my thirtieth birthday, framed by the only thing that stood me true that year: the sayings of my beloved grandmother. She was a woman from the traditional South, the kind of black woman for whom living and common sense were inextricable. I can't count the times her wisdom about life and love was my flashlight when one of my life's thunderstorms had knocked out the electricity. And even though Grandma is gone, her "mother wit" still inspires and guides me. It reminds me not to take my own dramas too seriously, to live life and not just get through it, to laugh a little and maybe, along the way, find true love. And in case I was prone to forget, it also reminds me that finding Prince Charming can mean kissing a lot of toads—not to mention some wicked cold sores.

Every Friday Night

"It's all beautiful till

somebody loses an eye"

1

GAL (Getting A Life)

How it all started

My grandmother always liked to say, "Everybody's got to roll around the floor one time real good." She also liked the old chestnut, "Only thing to do when a horse throws you is get right back on." I liked the sound of those two, but I never really considered what they meant until I had to live them—and the day came when I had to.

Before meeting Nicholas I'd never really given much thought to marriage. From high school to grad school, books and boys never carried equal weight—dating was strictly for entertainment. So his proposal took me by surprise, though when I thought about it, it seemed like a natural progression: We'd dated for two years, we had a great time together, and he had the makings of a good provider. He didn't do drugs or drink too much, he believed in God, and our families got along. So why not? Well, one clear October morning about six months before the wedding, the pit of my gut answered that question (and no, it wasn't PMS).

I suddenly wondered where was the chocolate buzz of being "in love"? Wasn't the earth supposed to move, or at least a few violins play? What about burning passion, or waves of desire? The knowledge in my heart that I had found my soul mate, my life partner, the love of my life? That morning I knew—maybe I was only twenty-four, but I knew that if we went through with it, we'd end up hating each other. So I called it quits. There was no high drama or nastiness: I called him and broke up with him, Fed-Exed the ring with a letter of apology, and that was that. Neat and clean.

Well, sort of. Over the next few years I sometimes felt a scary pang of regret. Was Nicholas my only chance for love? Had I bought into too many romance novels and movies with fairy-tale endings of what being with Mr. Right is supposed to sound, act, and feel like? I was really beginning to worry, but then, after three long years of unsuccessful dating and six months of halfhearted celibacy, I met Luke.

We had so much in common: the love of politics, jazz, good food and basketball, and an insatiable appetite for sex, not to mention the fireworks I saw every time we kissed. I thought he was fine—curly hair, skin the color of caramel, green eyes, chiseled jawline, six feet tall, muscular, and bowlegged. Our children would be beautiful. Okay, he didn't make six figures, have multiple degrees, or a sense of style when he wasn't in a suit. (He always wore green jeans—he thought they matched his eyes.) But he came from a hardworking, educated family, and was a "good" twenty-eight-year-old brother who made me feel like we were for keeps. Suddenly everything was clear: He was the one.

So what if he still had his ex-girlfriend's cat when we started dating, and had a near seizure every time he thought he saw her? So what if he went out with "women friends" when I was out of town on business—they were "just friends," and people can have friends outside of their relationship, right?

Besides love conquers all, right?

My Grandmother used to say, "God don't like ugly and ain't crazy about beauty." And damn if Luke didn't go and prove her right. The universe is brutally fair, and I couldn't help but think that the pain I caused Nicholas was coming back to haunt me. The fairy tale took only nine months to unravel. First, I found distinctly female jewelry in his desk drawer. "My sister left it last time she came over." Next was the box of K-Y in the trash. He swore it came in a giveaway bag from a conference and he'd thrown it away while cleaning when I was out of town. Finally, there was the condom in the toilet. He'd been caught and seemed relieved. I was unyielding. I gave him an ultimatum. He refused. It was over. I could only cry.

For weeks I refused to believe it had happened. I acted like a complete fool-ass—crying, not eating, not sleeping, walking by his house, calling his friends, his family, telling anyone who'd listen about how he'd done me wrong. I still couldn't believe the man I'd chosen would do this to me. How could this happen?

As a child of the 1970s, I was raised to believe that the

world was my oyster—I could have it all. Being an African-American woman was no longer a life sentence of disrespect, heartache, overwork, and underpay. The world was a different place now, and sistas could do it for themselves. Nobody came right out and said this, but the message was clear that if I earned degrees from "good schools," worked hard, followed the Ten Commandments, saved my money, respected my body, and prayed daily, I'd reap life's rewards: a good job and the pick of the litter. I managed to get the great job. But where was my pick?

I've been told that it takes about half the time a relationship lasts to get over it, but after the third month of continuous moping with no end in sight, my close friends had had enough—they never trusted Mr. Greenjeans anyway. I was depressed and it was beyond the circle of sistas—I needed God or therapy. Max, Kay, and Olga, in consultation with my big sister Bea, decided on therapy and scheduled an appointment for me—on a Friday night.

Now I was rattled enough at being sent to therapy (not that I didn't need it) by the people I trusted most, but Friday nights were *our* night—Max, Kay, Olga, and mine—and those Friday nights were the only thing that gave me any comfort. Kay and Olga are my sista-girls (Kay from college, Olga from grad school), truly sisters to me when Bea wasn't around. We somehow got in the habit of doing dinner and a video on Friday nights.

Max, the lone male in the pack . . . well, Max is a different story. The two of us had become "boys" in grad school: We crammed together, procrastinated by watching Saturday college football together, drowned our thesis blues at Dallas BBQ together, people-watched in Washington Square Park together, and, halfway into our second year, slept together.

Big mistake.

One stressed-out pre-exam night, a hug turned into a kiss and the kiss turned into—everything else. After about a month of avoidance and weirdness we vowed never to cross that line again, and happily went back to being "boys." Instead of ruining the friendship, it strengthened it. Having a close friend of the opposite sex to give dating advice and be a surrogate date for parties is just too valuable to sacrifice for something as potentially uncertain as sex. So soon after the Friday dinner-and-video night became a regular thing, I invited Max to become an honorary sista, the only man we allowed to infiltrate the circle. And he repaid the honor. He introduced Olga to her husband (his line brother from college), helped Kay get an apartment in his building, and showed us he was true blue in a hundred ways that helped us think of him as a "friend" first and a "man" second.

Friday nights became precious quality downtime for the four of us. We'd make dinner together and talk our way through the video, each of us recapping our week and getting feedback. For the newly engaged Olga, Friday nights were a chance to feel that she still had a life beyond the impending wedding and future hubby. Kay, queen of the dating game (and a *Rules* girl to boot), was only on a quest for Mr. Right. Her theory was that unavailability on a Friday night makes you more attractive to would-be suitors. And Max just loved kicking back with three beautiful women on a Friday night— without the stress of romance.

But the first few months after the breakup, I didn't "Thank God It's Friday" anymore—I wince just remembering it, but I think I spoiled a dozen Friday nights in a row, ranting, weeping, or just moping. But now Friday night was therapy night, and it gave me something constructive to do with all my unbearable feelings: I saved them up for the end of the week, then vented them for fifty straight minutes of tears and rage. *Then* I'd go and join my friends, and try not to be a zombie for the rest of the night.

I saw my therapist every Friday night for nearly six months, and thought we were making progress. I no longer pictured myself causing Luke permanent bodily harm, even if my weekly howling sessions were training me to take over the local chapter of the She-Woman Man-Haters' Club. Until one Friday night, as I was winding down an hour-long sob, the therapist asked, "So what's your firm's mental health leave policy?"

I was dumbfounded.

"We've been working together for nearly six months, and your depression seems to be worsening."

She just said my "depression." She thinks I'm clinically depressed—a wackadoo, a pathetic, heartbroken woman. Was she right?

"Perhaps you should be seeing a psychiatrist who could prescribe . . ."

Oh no. I wasn't listening anymore. I managed to schedule another appointment, mumbling, "I'll think about it," and got out of her office. That's it, I thought. I'll be damned if I'll let Luke make me spend the rest of my life on Prozac! Walking out into the brisk early March night air down Broadway towards Seventy-second Street, a surge of energy and clarity came over me. *He's* not crying. *He's* not in therapy. No one's telling *him* to go on Prozac. *He's* not taking a temporary vow of chastity while he gets himself together—he's already living with the next one. All he ever did was cheat and lie, so was I the one who deserved to be on meds?

HELL NO!

On the way home from the train, fuming at the prospect of being medicated to pull me out of the deep funk I'd been thrown into by a relationship I'd chosen to be in, I made a resolution: It was time to GAL again—to get a life. Yeah, yeah, great idea, but how?

By following my grandmother's advice: I was going to get back on that horse, and take back my Friday nights—hell, I was gonna take back my life. Was I ready? No. Was I determined? Yes. Did I keep my resolution? Damn skippy!

Armed with grandmother wit and the determination to get a life, I took a sabbatical from "friend/video night" and decided that for the next year I would spend my Friday nights dating, not feeling sorry for myself. In the course of that year I managed to "date" twenty-eight different men, averaging at least a date a week—I actually went out with sixteen of the twenty-eight more than twice. What you're about to read is the story of that year and those dates. It's also the story of what I learned, what I lost, and what I found.

2

Psycho

My Grandma always said . . .
Crazy is as crazy does

Resolve creates results, so my first date came to me thanks to Bea, who had dutifully told our whole entire family each and every nasty detail of Mr. Greenjeans's departure. As soon as Uncle Phil heard, he called from Los Angeles.

"Girl, you're young, bright, and beautiful. You need to get over that trifling Negro and get on with it. What did you do when you were seven and you busted your ass roller-skating down the hill?"

Here we go with the pep talk. "I got up."

"Well, hell—get on up now! Oh, wait—I got something for you. Hold on . . ."

Uncle Phil had someone to introduce me to, via conference call.

"Bill's a good brother: ivy degrees, 180 IQ, worth a few million, under thirty, and he's in the city on business." After twenty years on the West Coast, Uncle Phil still called New York "the city" like there was only one in the world. "You should meet him for a drink at least. We're talking future husband material. Now hold on a second—"

Click-click.

"Hey, I got my niece who lives in the city on the line. You're in the city—you guys should hang out."

And when did I become the welcome wagon for stray brothers visiting the city?

After I hung up, Uncle Phil and Bill arranged for us to meet the following week at The Shark Bar Restaurant (the spot for the profiling crowd—known for the occasional star sighting, but the collard greens are almost as good as my grandmother's). Uncle Phil knew that if nothing else, I'd enjoy the food. When Bill called the next day to confirm our date, he seemed nice enough, but . . .

Mistake 1 I agreed to oblige my uncle.

Mistake 2 I dressed up—tailored black suit with skirt to show off my legs—and had hair and nails done. I should've gone for the housedress and doo-rag look, and just scared him off.

Mistake 3 He was thirty minutes late.

On first sight I stiffened—he was a mud-duck. Now a mud-duck is a guy you don't find attractive right away, but if you stick around, and don't look too hard, you'll find something endearing enough to convince you to be seen in public with him. I decided it was his lips. Still, Uncle Phil was gonna have to produce some Knicks tickets to make up for this one.

His conversational skills weren't bad, and he was smart enough to know I was there as a favor to my uncle. One glass of wine turned into three, and then an invitation to dinner.

Mistake 4 I accepted.

Mistake 5 He started discussing his ex-wife—a detail my uncle missed—and his eighteen-month nervous breakdown.

Before the main course arrived, I heard about the courtship, the wedding, the marriage, her two miscarriages, the divorce, the settlement, and the current custody arrangement for their Scottish terrier. By the time the plates hit the table I was already working out my exit strategy. I'd go to the ladies' room and set my pager to go off in fifteen minutes, feign a work emergency, and disappear in a puff of smoke. As the details emerged about his failed attempt to kill his father, wiretapping his ex-wife's phone, and hiring a private investigator to track her down after she fled across the country with the terrier, fifteen minutes was feeling like fifteen years. Forget Knicks tickets, Uncle Phil—we're talking weekend package to Rio!

His lips curled and contorted as he told his story. Then it got worse. He started trembling, wringing his napkin, rolling his eyes, and taking deep breaths just this side of hyperventilation. If this man turns into the Hulk, Uncle Phil will have to die.

Retreating to the ladies' room, I discovered that I'd set my pager on military time—so much for my magical exit. I did my best, though: I came back to the table, told him the beeper had gone off, and said I'd have to skip dessert and run back to the office.

He gave me an understanding nod, saying something about how "Sure, it happens to me all the time." As I extended my hand to thank him for dinner, he grabbed it and pulled me toward him. By reflex I pulled away just as hard, nearly knocking down the couple at the table behind us. While everyone collected themselves and apologized, I grabbed my coat, hailed a cab, and made a clean getaway.

I called Bea as soon as I got home, to check in and relay the evening's events. "Uncle Phil set me up with a Psycho." As only an older, wiser sister can do, she put it all in perspective. "Better to be out with a Psycho than become a psycho. Good to see you're trying to get a life." Sisterly love—ya gotta love it.

3

Monopolizers

My Grandma always said . . .
Just cause they wink and blink
at you doesn't mean they
mean you any good.

You're at a party, you see him and you can't take your eyes off each other. When you meet he's polite and respectful, and just a little flirty. He makes you feel attractive. You exchange numbers and he actually calls within two or three days. How refreshing! Then he calls again—every day. Before you can drop a hint or even ask him yourself, he's inviting you out, remembering the things you've mentioned enjoying—maybe lunch at a new café, roller-blading in the park, a jazz concert. Nothing too romantic, mind you, just pleasant activities to get to know each other. He seems like a nice guy and of course all men can't be psychos, dogs, players, and commitment-phobes. Can they? There are some wonderful men in the world, and maybe this is the end of kissing frogs—at least for now.

But then one Friday night when the two of you have an activity planned, a friend calls to invite you to do something fun—maybe cocktails or a dinner party. Naturally, you accept you haven't hung out with your friends in a while because you've been busy taking care of business or (it hits you) hanging out with him. Besides, you think it's time for your friends to meet the mystery man.

When he calls to confirm, you mention your friend's gathering and how it's the perfect chance for him to meet the other people in your life. There's a long pause, followed by what sounds like a slight whine. "I thought Friday nights were our time together."

You're a little surprised and you say, "But we will be together!"

Now you can practically hear him pout. "Well, if you'd rather see them instead of me, I guess we'll get together another time."

You shift from being surprised to being angry. "Are you saying you don't want me to see my friends?"

He gets what he's done wrong and tries to assuage you. In the tone of an indulgent uncle he says, "Tell you what—let's meet as planned and then play it by ear." (Trust me: You'll never make it to the gathering.)

Suddenly it hits you. You're with a Monopolizer! Surprised? Don't be.

The problem with most monopolizers is that they're actually good guys at heart—very few of them are consciously trying to dominate your life, isolate you from the world, amputate your arms and legs, and keep you in a box. Chances are they're trying to do a bit of replacement therapy. Sometimes they have recently broken up with someone—like a couple of months ago—and they're still processing the breakup. They're determined to find someone new, but they're not interested in doing the bar scene or chasing women in general.

They're just needy, and they have to be seeing someone exclusively to feel like they're whole. All they want is one woman to spend all their free time with. Is that so wrong?

But there were clues along the way. There always are.

Case in point: Marco and I met phone banking two nights before Election Day. We went out for dinner with the rest of the group of young politically minded phone bankers. We chatted, laughed, flirted, and of course at the end of the evening exchanged phone numbers. A webmaster for a small company, his schedule gave him most evenings and weekends free. First, the nightly calls started. Then the weekly outings: brunch at the Potbelly Café, jazz at Small, a day at MoMA, ice-skating in Prospect Park, and tea and German chocolate cake at Brooklyn Moon. Things were going along nicely—lots of attention, hand-holding, pleasantly gentle kisses goodnight, and tender embraces that ended before I had to wriggle away. I was digging him—until his business trip out west.

We talked until the wee hours of the morning as he packed for his trip. He called from the airport before his flight boarded. He called at the airport when he reached his destination. He called after he checked into the hotel. He called after his first meeting, after lunch, before dinner, and after dinner. Of course these were all two-minute conversations:

Hey, just wanted to let you know I've arrived.
Hey, calling to see how your day is going.

Hey, I was thinking about you.
Hey, how about dinner together on Friday when I get back?
Hey, what time will you be home tonight?

Okay, it's the first day of a weeklong trip, you talk all the time, and he's having a little separation anxiety. You think, oh, this is cute—he misses me. But by the third day of this, it's not so cute anymore. It seems like you're talking to him every three hours or so, and there's a reason for that: you are. You begin screening all your calls, at work and at home. You return the after-dinner call. Of course he's perturbed, but you explain that things are crazy in the office right now. He should understand, right?

We agreed that I'd pick him up from JFK and we'd go to Jackson Diner for the best Indian food outside of the subcontinent. At baggage claim, he hugged me so hard I could barely breathe, and kissed me like I'd come back from the dead. I've never been a big fan of PDA under the best of circumstances, and I must have shown it because he sulked the entire ride from the airport. After the waiter took our order, Marco whipped out a legal-size piece of paper with a calendar for the next six months. He had planned activities for us—for every weekend, and two evenings each week. This trip had given him clarity. He wanted to spend as much time as he could with me. Perhaps in a few months we'd move in together.

Now hold on—for the record, let me tell you that at this point we hadn't had so much as a slumber party, let alone sex. But besides that, I'm a woman who treasures her solitude. Ask Max, Bea, Kay, or Olga—they'll tell you that I cherish time alone as much as cats love sitting on windowsills.

But Marco wasn't interested in that. He wasn't trying to

hear how I had experienced the past week of our being apart. He didn't seem to get that time alone and apart is healthy for all relationships, and that people need to have activities separate from each other for a relationship to remain healthy.

"Look, Marco," I said. "A strong relationship is not about merging identities!"

He gave me a look of horror, like I'd just blasphemed. If he'd been carrying a vial of holy water, I'm sure he would have thrown it at me. The conversation didn't get better from there.

When we got to his house he invited me to spend the night. I declined as politely as I could, but that only incited a tirade about my being a prude, cynical about love, and ultimately uncaring.

That was it—he had just stomped on my last nerve. I told him in no uncertain terms that it was in his best interest to get out of my car and not to call me again. But, of course, he called. And called. And called. And he probably would have kept calling, until the Friday night that Lance answered my phone.

4

Free to Be You

and Me

My Grandma always said . . .
If you make your bed hard,
you'll have to lie in it.

Oh, he was fine—Pretty-Ricky fine. He could've been a Ford model, staring at you from a Tommy Hilfiger or Ralph Lauren ad. But he wasn't. Lance was a Morehouse College man, now in law school, with a solid reputation as a world-class ho.

It was a Friday night and I was at the Metronome. A restaurant that turned nightclub toward midnight (kind of like a vampire), the place guaranteed at least five hours of over-priced drinks, deafening hip-hop and ol' school R&B for work-weary folks wanting to hang out, dance, drink, and potentially find someone for the night. The music and the chat were both feeling trite when he glided over to the bar. Lucky for me, he was hanging out with Sam, a friend of a friend. Sam introduced us and bought a round. After a bit of small talk, I thanked Sam for the drink and gave him a hug; then I winked at Lance, slid him my business card, and disappeared into the crowd.

Sunday afternoon he left a message and his number on my office voice mail, along with an invitation to hang out later in the week. I returned the call, and we made a plan for the following Friday night. It would be an ambitious evening of cocktailing starting at Match, and proceeding to the Bowery Bar, Mekka, Izzy's, and late night at BOB's. With so much happening so quickly I decided it was time to run a background check.

I called Kay, who knew him when she was on exchange at Spelman College during his Morehouse years, and then Olga, whose ex-boyfriend was in his law school class. All the reconnaissance said the same thing: He was a ho, he would probably always be a ho, and was having no trouble maintaining his reputation as a ho among his fellow law school students. But he was articulate, at a top law school and, most important, a dead ringer for Tyson Beckford.

Even though I knew I was dealing with a consummate gamer, the excitement of the challenge—and my libido—suspended all common sense. We went lounge-hopping and had a blast. His kiss goodnight is still unrivaled. I was in lust. I've always maintained that no sex is better than bad sex, so it was months since anyone had turned me on enough to schedule a bikini waxing. But this, as I expected, was far from bad.

Three weeks went by after our date, but I was so busy I barely noticed. I'd been consumed with work, and I was spending at least three nights a week traveling on business. The phone was ringing as I unlocked the door to my apartment. It was Lance—he wanted to make a home-cooked meal and help me relax. I dropped my suitcase and told him I'd be there in an hour.

I tore through the apartment with Erykah Badu (my getting dressed music) playing in the background, and damned if I couldn't find my newly purchased Miracle Bra and Victoria's Secret thong. I showered, shaved, perfumed, checked for ash, brushed my teeth, did my hair, and applied my makeup, all in a record twenty minutes. Then I took five long minutes of deliberation before deciding on a long-sleeved black V-necked cashmere sweater and jeans—this was no time to hide my assets.

Two Cornish game hens and three bottles of wine later, he ran me a peppermint bath, followed with a lavender-oil body and foot massage. This was the ultimate antidote to business travel! Kissing led to sucking, and sucking led to . . . you know the rhyme. The only glitch came during pillow talk, when he almost ruined the moment by whispering, "I want to know the *real* you, if only for tonight." It sounded so much like a bad Luther line that I decided to ignore it.

That night turned into a few months of late night anatomical study sessions, midday brown-bag lunch breaks, and early evening cocktails. He was a plentiful source of wonderful sex, and we never discussed what was going on between us. I saw him when I saw him.

People's actions usually tell you all you need to know about them, and Lance's actions told me he was a classic Mr. Right Now, a man of the moment. And our moment was about to end.

First he stood me up for a movie he suggested. A week later

he left a two-minute message about an ailing grandmother. I guess he forgot he told me all his grandparents were dead, and had been since he was six. I "forgot" to call him back. Weeks went by and I didn't hear from him. I missed him a lot less than I missed the sex.

It was another Friday night and I was out as usual. I was at Red Strip when I saw him. He was there with my friend Kay's summer associate, grinding her into the dance floor like a drill bit. He saw me and released her from his undulating hips. I gave him a nod, turned my back to him, and ordered a drink.

An hour later as I waited in line for the bathroom (too many Red Stripes), he sheepishly walked up and leaned forward to kiss me on the cheek. "I know this looks shady, but I have attachment issues. I was starting to develop memories with you, and I'm too young for—"

I cut him off before he could finish. "Whoa, boy. Didn't we agree that we were all free to be you and me?"

I guess he didn't expect my response because he visibly wilted. I had to smile. Nothing beats out-gaming a gamer— and who said I was lonely, anyway? Didn't he notice I was there with the Marauder?

5

The Marauders—

Subliminal Seduction

My Grandma always said . . .
You can do bad all by yourself.

I didn't want to go to Olga's wedding, but as one of her closest friends and a bridesmaid I didn't really have a choice: friendship brings certain obligations. And she'd bent over backwards to be sensitive to my ailing heart throughout the whole planning process, and included me only strategically. Whenever I asked if she needed my help, she'd say, "What am I paying the wedding planner for?" Secretly I was glad. The thought of picking out a wedding gown and all the other bridal stuff that goes along with it would have reminded me of how far away I was from ever getting to the altar. Sure, I'd managed to date, but a boyfriend, let alone a committed relationship, seemed farther away than becoming President of the United States.

It's lucky for me that crying at weddings is considered appropriate. I'm sure everyone thought my tears were about how transcendently happy the couple looked and how wonderful love is, but I'm sorry to say that all the salt water I shed was really selfishly, narcissistically, for me. I couldn't help wondering if my day would ever come; or for that matter how being in love with someone could feel so incredible at one point and so awful at another. I managed to pull myself together before anyone suspected, reminding myself this day wasn't about me, it was Olga's wedding day, and she had finally found someone worthy of her. Tomorrow I could wallow all I wanted, but I'd make the best of today.

Fate likes a cruel joke as much as anybody, which is why it arranged for me to catch the bouquet. A sign that maybe there was hope for me after all? I didn't know, but I danced the evening away, and managed to have a good time despite myself.

Olga called when she and Claude returned from their honeymoon in Bali.

"You know, you were a hit at the wedding. People have been asking about you. Remember Scott who I used to work with? He was checking you out. Can I give him your number or your e-mail? Never mind, I'll set it up—we'll have dinner on Friday, and it'll be a double date. It's done."

"Wait, wait, wait. Wait a second. He's an adult, isn't he? Why didn't he say anything to *me*? He didn't even ask me to dance. There were other guys who had no problem chatting with me or asking me to dance, especially after I caught your bouquet."

"Don't be so harsh. He's a little shy. And you never know. People meet their mates in the strangest ways."

"Olga, shy works when you're seven. How old is he?"

"Girl—"

"All right, okay, I'll do it. For you." *And besides, who knows—maybe he's the one . . .*

As I scurried through the door of Patria, I saw her at the bar with an exceptionally handsome man in a suit. My first thought was *Hmm, a possibility . . .*

Claude's flight from L.A. had been delayed, so it was just Olga, Scott, and me. She introduced us. I didn't remember him from the wedding, but seeing him now I thought he was definitely worth remembering. His smile and eyes seemed to radiate. He reminded me of a little boy who couldn't wait to tell a secret. He was charming, thoughtful, and not self-absorbed— I imagined Uncle Phil calling him "a gentleman and a scholar."

Throughout dinner Olga kept dropping items from each of our vitas, and telling stories about how the other lived a full and interesting life. With a gaze and a wink, we mutually acknowledged that we were Olga's latest matchmaking victims. But when she excused herself immediately after dinner, saying she had to meet her hubby, we were left on the sidewalk, staring at each other awkwardly.

Being a gentleman, he presented me with several options: He could hail me a cab, we could head to Yaffa Tea Room for dessert, or we could stroll to Lemon for cigars and port. I like a good port and a Cuban cigar as much as the next gal, but I opted for the tearoom. Is cigar breath really an aphrodisiac?

As the evening became late night, we talked about politics, sociology, philosophy, spirituality, and creation . . . and agreed to see each other again. He called a car for me, and kissed me good night—on the cheek.

The next day Olga was beside herself. "See? I told you! I knew you two would hit it off!"

Jazz at Iridium, Roy Hargrove, Cyrus Chestnut, Alvin Ailey, bowling, shooting pool, making dinners together, Blockbuster nights, reading the Sunday *New York Times* together, a weekend in Chicago, reading each other Nikki Giovanni's *Love Poems* . . . we had days and nights and weeks of fun and sheer comfort. Little by little, I found myself thinking Olga might have been right. It felt so good just being with him, and it seemed like he was feeling it, too.

Then one evening while I was chopping red onions for a potato salad and humming along to Billie Holiday, he embraced me from behind and held me. I felt him take a deep breath, and as I turned to face him I saw tears rolling down his cheeks. At first I thought it was the onions, but then he cried quietly for almost an hour, never answering my questions about what was wrong, and I stopped pushing. In that moment, I understood that tears don't always need a conversation. We hardly said a word during dinner, just holding hands across the table and smiling when our eyes met. We fell asleep intertwined. As I dozed off, I thought, "This is real intimacy. He's opening up to me. It won't be easy, but we'll work it through . . . together." When I woke up the next morning, he was gone. There was a note on the table:

> Thanks for making the last few months incredible.
> I'm moving to Portland today, and didn't know
> how to tell you. Someday I'll repay you.

I doubt it. When the Marauder left, he didn't just take a piece of my heart; he took the $100 from my wallet, a stack of my CDs, *and* my portable disc player.

6

Diminishing Returns—

One Drink Too Many

My Grandma always said . . .
If you find it in the gutter,
throw a rug over it
and keep going

My grandmother liked to tell me,
especially after I moved to New York, that God
watches out for babies and fools. Paying hom-
age to the porcelain goddess and promising God
and my grandmothers in the afterlife that I
wouldn't consume more than three alcoholic
drinks in one sitting never really drove home
what a fool *too* much drink can turn you into.
But meeting Stuart did.

The week had enough drama for a Jerry
Springer Show.

SATURDAY AND SUNDAY: I worked all weekend to meet a Monday morning deadline, only to get slammed in the meeting.

MONDAY EVENING: After bitching to Bea for an hour, I regrouped and prepped for a Tuesday meeting in Chicago with a 6:00 A.M. flight.

TUESDAY EVENING: Flew back to New York and went straight to the office, where I worked until 10:00 P.M.

WEDNESDAY MORNING: In the office at 7:30 A.M. to prep for afternoon meeting. During the meeting the client changes the entire deal structure, which has to be completed before noon on Friday.

WEDNESDAY EVENING: Meeting ends at 6:00 P.M. and I start redoing the analysis. I'm handed another assignment that has to be completed before a 10:00 A.M. conference call on Thursday, the next day.

THURSDAY MORNING: After two hours of sleep, I'm back in the office at 8:00 A.M. to find out that half of the quick-turnaround assignment is dead and the new sections won't be e-mailed until 6:00 P.M., but the new sections have to be incorporated into the analysis, which is now due Friday morning.

THURSDAY EVENING: I stay in the office all night to complete both assignments by Friday morning, which I do.

FRIDAY MORNING: 10:30 A.M. the computer server crashes.

FRIDAY AFTERNOON: At 12:30 P.M. the server comes back up, but the copier jams, and it seems like the entire tech support group has gone to lunch or left for the weekend.

FRIDAY AFTERNOON: From 2:00 to 3:30 P.M., first meeting.

FRIDAY AFTERNOON TO EARLY EVENING: From 4:00

to 6:30 P.M., second meeting, assignments completed, but the bags under my eyes make me look like a raccoon on heroin.

FRIDAY EVENING: By 7:00 P.M. my bed is calling my name, but Kay and Max both have left voice mails for me to join them at Pageant for a cocktail.

After a week like that, I figured a quick cocktail at Pageant with fellow stress victims would be a great way to start the weekend and still be home in time to fall asleep watching *20/20* at 10:00 P.M.

Pageant, a gathering place for the briefcase-toting and the suit-clad, is the ideal after-work spot for numbing one's brain with its 6:00 to 8:00 open bar, usually sponsored by some liquor company seeking to infiltrate the "urban" professional market. Everyone there is running to or from something: the pressures of trying to climb the corporate ladder; working eighteen-hour days and coming home to an empty overpriced apartment and another evening of leftover take-out; realizations that we're all closer to forty than twenty; trying not to be the oldest man or woman in the club. Some may even be searching for a possible love connection.

But by 8:00 P.M. at Pageant the woes of the week are a thing of the past, like Members Only jackets and Sassoon jeans. By 8:00 P.M. a line snakes down the block and around the corner with wannabes or supposed-to-be VIPs cutting the line and saying they're on the list (there is no list). By 8:00 P.M. the elixir of the evening and the latest pulsating beat combine to create the haze that makes taste, dignity, and standards seem like arcane ideology. The corporate uniforms of navy blue three-button suits and blue shirts make the most physically unattractive male look like a power broker, and the more attractive look like Denzel Washington on Oscar night.

Kay and Max met me at the upstairs bar. "You look wrecked." Max took my shoulders and inspected me. "What the hell are they doing to you over there?"

"I don't want to talk about it."

"Oh! Well then, what's your poison for tonight? Johnny and ginger? Or you going for the hard stuff?"

Drinking dulls the awareness of being in a place with people not only my mother would find questionable. Drink one takes off the edge of the day. Drink two helps relax the inhibitions. Drink three usually facilitates acting like a fool-ass and the beginnings of the living illustration of the economic principle of marginal utility. Defined as the satisfaction from consuming a little more of a good or service, with the marginal costs being the cost to produce another unit or increment of that good or service, marginal utility has a point where incremental cost brings diminishing returns (I *told* you I went to graduate school!). As it relates to the drinking and the dating scene, that cost often comes in the form of giving someone your phone number when your common sense is impaired by several glasses of some liquid anesthetic. In your right mind, you'd run far and fast in the opposite direction. But as Jay-Z thumped and my three drinks turned into five, my right mind and I weren't even in the same neighborhood.

Before I knew it, it was ten o'clock and the after-work crowd had transformed itself into the Friday-night-out crowd. The worries and wariness of the week were gone. My only cares were whether I wanted to dance to the next song and if the man dancing with me would stop trying to carry on a conversation while stepping on my Ferragamo pumps and mashing my already aching feet. I felt it was time to go when Max grabbed my waist. "I know," I said. "Time to go home—I'm fading fast."

"Oh, no you're not, little Miss Twinkletoes. Looks like

you've had significant fun already, and you're just about to start having a good time. Come on over to the table and meet Stu. He's been asking about you all evening. And be nice—he just broke up with his girlfriend."

"Aren't I always nice?"

"Aw, *hell* no! You know how you can be, Evilene."

"So are you trying to hook a sista up?"

"NO." Max was emphatic. "Everybody's grown—I'm just doing introductions. Handle your business."

I swam after Max through a sea of bobbing brown bodies—the most I'd seen all week—some still in work gear, others in the hangout uniform of all black. At the table, Kay stood guard over a round of lemon shots decorating the table. "We've been waiting for you, little Miss Solid Gold Dancer. Bottoms up!"

"Yeah, we've been waiting for you." Just as I noticed the slight slur in his voice, the stranger spilled a bit of his lemon shot on me. His tie was off, his shirt was wrinkled like he'd just picked it off the floor, and he reeked of vodka.

Max looked disgusted. "Oh, um, this is Stuart." He grimaced an apology at me.

"Yeah, I'm Stuart and you sure are . . ." For a second I thought he was doing a drunken sailor routine, but no, it was no routine. "Excuse me—don't go away. I'll be right back." He stumbled off towards the bathroom.

"Max, I know I've had a few myself, but it looks like your boy can't handle his liquor."

Kay chimed in. "There is *nothing* worse then a sloppy drunk man."

"Oh yes there is. How about a sloppy drunk man trying to carry on a sloppy drunk conversation with you while he showers you with his bad liquor breath?"

"Aw, come on now, ladies. I told you he just broke up with his girl. You've both been there. Cut him some slack."

"Some slack my ass." Kay wasn't having him. "Do you know *why* they broke up?" Before anyone could answer, "I'll tell you why. A drunken man's mind is a sober man's tongue. He's got that stupid male checklist in his head and girlie was never gonna have a check mark on every line. After five years she figured out there weren't any diamonds coming her way and pulled the plug, and now 'he's' all broken up. Typical— too little, too late. Serves him right to have the blues."

Max and I had to laugh. "So tell us how you *really* feel!"

"Listen," I said, "I think I've had more fun than I can stand for one night. I don't have to go home but I got to get the hell out of here. Anyone up for grub? I need something to absorb all this alcohol."

Kay was halfway to the door. "Now that's the best idea I've heard all day—let's go to Around the Clock. Max, are you bringing Staggering Stu?"

He gave a guess-I-have-to nod. "Let's go, Evilenes."

When we walked the couple of blocks to Around the Clock, Stu seemed to have sobered up a bit, but it was short-lived. First he harassed the server. "So what would you do for a hundred dollar tip?" Next it was the NYU students sitting across from us. "College is about experiences—don't you want to experience me?"

Kay talked to Max through her teeth. "You'd best get your boy before somebody else does."

Max leaned over and tried to be subtle. "Stu, you're making an ass out of yourself. Chill."

"I'm just having some fun. I'm a free man."

Kay didn't think so. "Yeah, you're free all right, but you're about to be in lockdown if you don't stop harassing people, and we're not getting you out of jail. Act like you have some home training."

Before Stu could put together a response, the food arrived and saved us all some grief because for a brief time conversation besides "Pass the ketchup" ceased: Burgers and fries at 1:00 A.M. is the best cure for impending hangovers. But the downside is post-ethnic dining syndrome, the desire to conk out immediately afterward. Still, everyone managed to maintain some level of decorum, except Stu: his head, dropped back and he began snoring—loudly, like a lumberjack's buzz saw. To make things worse, deep sleep was about to set in. I was afraid that at any minute we would be treated to the sight of a string of spit falling in slow motion from his open mouth.

Max looked away, and we both started laughing. "Where did you find him? No wonder his girlfriend broke up with him!"

Stu nodded so hard I was sure he would fall forward and hit his head on the table, but he woke up instead, with a bleary blink. "Was I snoring?"

Kay grabbed her bag. "Get the check. Let's go."

But we still had the cab ride back to Brooklyn. Max took shotgun, and Stu insisted on sitting between me and Kay since he'd be the last one out of the cab. Neither of us thought what a bad move that was until it was too late. Before we reached the Manhattan Bridge he released a silent but deadly fart. Our windows went down and we stuck our noses out as far as they could go, like a couple of well-coiffed purebreds. Then mid-bridge Stu tried to crawl across Kay, struggling to reach the window; but he missed, and threw up all over her. Just the sound of him hurling made me and Max wince, and we let out a collective "Ughhh!" But Kay was moved to new heights of eloquence.

"Are you in college? Are you in high school? You nasty, weak, no-liquor-holding, shouldn't-be-let-out-of-the-house-let-alone-into-a-bar, dis*gus*ting, no-home-training, nasty rat bastard mother*fucker*!"

By now Stu had fallen to the floor of the cab. "I'm so sorry," he mumbled, "so sorry, so sorry, so sorry," like it was his mantra. That just gave Kay more fuel for the fire.

"Yep, that's right, you're sorry—a sorry excuse for a man! Sorry you're getting my dry cleaning bill is what you're gonna be—and you *better* hope this shit comes out, or you're buying it!"

We got to Kay and Max's building a couple of minutes later, but it still wasn't soon enough for Stu, who threw up again just as Kay was getting out, barely missing the back of her legs. She ran off into the building with a loud "UGGGGH!!!"

Max pulled Stu out and went to pay the cabbie, who swore in a language I hadn't heard before. I decided to walk the last few blocks home.

"Max, handle your boy and be sure you call Kay and apologize. Talk to her." He just shook his head, all his energy going into keeping Stu upright. "Feel better Stu."

Stu muttered something, and sat down on the curb.

I felt a little bad for him. He might be a decent guy, but at age thirty he hadn't figured out that one drink too many won't cure the heartbreak of a breakup, or the worries of the workweek. One thing alcohol *will* do if you're not careful is make you act like a baby *and* a fool; it could even end you up in the gutter.

"Put a snake in your bosom

and it'll bite you"

7

"If You Have to Ask, Then You're Not on My Level"

My Grandma always said . . .
Don't count your chickens
before they hatch.

One Friday night Kay and I agreed to meet at Barnes & Noble in Union Square to pick up some books and then grab dinner at Punch. Neither of us had a Friday night date, and we weren't up for another Black Diamonds party at the Exchange Club. Every Friday night Black Diamonds, the young, upwardly mobile urban professionals' source of entertainment, threw a party somewhere in the city; it always seemed like the same two-hundred brown folk were in attendance. But Kay's latest boy hadn't called by Wednesday to schedule and she didn't want to be tempted to call, or to accept an invitation if he happened to call while she was channel surfing.

In the magazine section on the second floor, Kay devoured the latest issues of all the fashion magazines while I busied myself with *National Geographic.*

"That's a hype issue. Be sure to check out the article on child slavery in the Sudan. That shit is mad deep."

I looked up at the guy next to me. The jeans hanging off his ass and Timberlands made him look like he was a week away from an orange jumpsuit. But, I thought, you can't *always* judge a book by its cover . . .

"Thanks," I said. "I'll be sure to do that."

"If you like that, check this out." He handed me a magazine I'd never seen before. "This really breaks it down. Gives a global deconstructionist perspective. It's too heavy, too progressive for most folks. Make you say, 'Hmmm.' You look like a deep sista. My name's Elliot, but my friends call me LL."

I snickered to myself. *Can't I go anywhere and be in peace? Men have no compunction about disturbing a woman by herself.*

"It's nice to meet you, Elliot."

"Oh, so we're not friends? You can call me LL, but that's all right, I like the way you say my name. I can tell you got class."

Oh here we go. I smiled, said "Thanks," and politely headed towards Kay.

"Girl, you pick up all types."

"I must have a sign on my forehead that says 'Please accost me. I'm a single black woman. Any man will do.' "

Kay glanced over at LL, who was still staring my way. "I don't see the sign, but I know *he* did. You hungry yet? There are only so many fashion magazines a girl can read." We decided Blue Water Grill would do more than Punch to boost our spirits. Not more than five minutes after being seated, in pimped Elliot. I tried to hide behind the menu, but to no avail: the maître d' sat him directly across from us. I refused to look his way.

Kay was in a mood. "Oh, look—isn't that the guy from Barnes & Noble?" She waved, but I didn't look to see if he waved back.

I talked to the wine list. "Don't encourage him. I just want to eat in peace." As I finished my sentence, the waiter appeared.

"Ladies, the gentleman across the room would like to send you a bottle of wine." Kay and I spoke at the same time.

ME: Tell him, "No, thank you."
SHE: Tell him, "Thank you!" How sweet! Which wine?
WAITER: "I'll ask. Pardon me."

"Kay don't encourage folks. That's how you always get in trouble."

"Don't be silly. He's grown and that's what a man is supposed to do if he's trying to get next to you."

"You've watched too many Marilyn Monroe movies. If we accept the wine, then when he comes over here we've *got* to talk to him."

"That's okay. He's kind of cute."

The waiter appeared with a bottle of South African Merlot. Kay nodded her approval and the waiter disappeared, but she was beside herself. Kay smirked. "He has decent taste."

"Hmmph!" I wasn't buying it—I'd actually heard the boy speak. "My money says the waiter suggested it."

The waiter reappeared with the open bottle and two

glasses, and gave the taste to Kay. "He has *better* than decent taste—this is great wine!"

I rolled my eyes.

"Give a brother a break. Just because he looks like he could be on Rikers or in some Nas video doesn't mean he is. You're such a priss sometimes. If he were in Brooks Brothers you'd be grinning from ear to ear, singing and swinging like Christmas."

"You're full of it, Miss No Capped Men."

"Now don't be a hater." Kay wagged her finger. "I know what I need, and I am very clear that I need someone who can provide for me. If a man is capped—limited earning potential, no bonus payout, no possibility of a golden parachute—then he might as well be on Social Security. I'm not saying he's got to be a doctor, lawyer, or banker. I'm just saying he's got to be industrious and understand that *his* role is to ante up." She raised her glass to our benefactor, and he raised his in return; I picked mine up a moment too late, just in time to feel foolish, but then I turned my attention back to Kay to make myself feel a little less foolish.

"I see. And so what exactly are *you* bringing to the table?"

"I'm thirty, fertile, fine, a size 6 with 36Cs." She straightened her posture as if she wanted to stretch her back, not show off her assets. "I'm also smart, and funny, *and* I have impeccable taste."

"Well, I'm sorry to have to break it to you if you hadn't noticed, but there's a whole lot of that running around New York City. What are you bringing to the table that a million other single women in this town *don't* have? Would *you* want to date you? Are you the person, in any way, shape, or form that *you* want to be with? Are *you* out there doing or being any of the things you'd want your significant other to do or be? I'm serious, Kay, no one in his right mind *wants* to financially support someone. That's a lot of pressure, and even if someone goes for it you'll *still* be paying a price."

Kay gave me an aw-shucks smile, like I'd just been praising her to the skies. It took me a second to realize that it wasn't for my benefit but for Mr. Jeans-Off-His-Ass; even so, she was unfazed. "If that's what it takes, then I'm with it. This career woman, working like a slave on a plantation just to bump your head on the glass-ceiling business is way overrated. I'll have to pay the piper one way or another, so it might as well have a diamond attached."

"Well, if that's—"

"Ladies, may I join you?" It was Elliot, Mr. Thug Life himself, but he was speaking a new language.

Kay was all teeth. "Please. The wine is a great choice. Thank you. Please sit down and have some."

"Thanks, it's one of my favorites. I visited the vineyard when I was there."

Kay now shifted into full flirt mode. "Really, South Africa? What was it like? When were you there?"

"This past winter. Of course, it was summer there. It's a beautiful country, with beautiful and kind people. I was volunteering with Doctors Without Borders."

What was I saying about books and their covers? To call him smart would be an hilarious understatement: He was bright, thoughtful, a rigorous thinker, sharply analytical, and at the same time deeply conscious. As we talked more, I realized that Elliot was one of those brothers who grew up in suburbia—Scarsdale, to be exact—and was still affirming his brownness. His adoption of thug-life gear and talk was his way of "keeping it real." He was perpetrating. Although he'd become an epidemiologist, the Harvard and Stanford degrees didn't really mean much to him, and he swore he hadn't bought into the New York buppie dream of the brownstone and the Beemer motorcycle—but he was living it. His diction, the BMW SUV, the brownstone, the two apartment buildings in Harlem, the globe-trotting, and the hanging with the high profile set blew his cover.

"Are you going to the Black Ski Summit? Hamptons or the Vineyard for Labor Day Weekend? Black Film Festival in Acapulco?"

As the waiter took our orders and eventually brought our meals, nothing slowed Elliot and Kay. They went back and forth, comparing parties, stores, restaurants, and the best of the best for the next hour plus. I ate my food and nodded when necessary, but mentally I'd long checked out of the conversation. *Send out laundry, move bookcase, find screwdriver in junk closet*—I was busy with an action-packed weekend ahead of me.

When the check came, he whipped out the platinum AMEX. "Ladies, please—allow me. This has been such a treat. It's the least I can do."

On top of the wine, this was just too much. "Come on. You don't know us from a can of paint. We cannot allow you to pay." Under the table Kay kicked me in the shin so hard I yelped.

Elliot laughed. "Forget about it. It's done."

Kay excused herself and went to the bathroom. He'd baited her throughout dinner, and as soon as she left the table he started a critique more thorough than any literary review.

"Your friend Kay is cool, but she's too caught up—too Eurocentric, too Brooks Brothers and Bloomingdale's, and no global perspective. There's more going on in the world than Puffy's latest video, or the new Gucci-whatever. All of us educated Negroes let ourselves be *mis*educated, and then we wonder why we're so unhappy. We've sold our souls for the good life, thinking we can buy our happiness with the almighty dollar, but there isn't enough cheddar in all the Kraft factories to put it back together."

"So what do you suggest? We all move into the projects? Or go back to Africa?"

"No, but we have to be more concerned with the least of our brethren. People do *not* give back. We're all so consumed with the material things that are supposed to give us an identity and status that we don't use our gifts, talents, and privilege to bring the rest of the community along."

"Um, don't you find it just a little ironic that we're having this conversation sitting up in the Blue Water Grill? And wasn't that a platinum card?"

He waved my remark away with a smile. "Like the ad says, 'membership has its privileges.' But that doesn't mean it can't be used for the good of the whole."

"Or to pick up women?" I was at a low simmer.

"*Touché*. So are you down for the cause? Or are you a social-stepping sista, too?"

Kay returned from the bathroom asking, "Anyone up for a nightcap at Lemon?"

Elliot declined, and Kay looked shocked. She obviously thought they'd made a connection, and he'd given her no reason to think otherwise.

On the way out the door Elliot took my arm. "You didn't answer my question."

Kay gave both of us a squinting look over her glasses like she'd been betrayed while in the bathroom.

I gave the man a coy smile. "Elliot, thank you for dinner. But brother, if you have to ask, then clearly we're not on the same level."

He let my arm go, shook his head, and walked toward the gleaming black SUV parked on the street.

8

The Orbiters

My Grandma always said . . .
The sun doesn't rise and set around
you . . . But if you ever think it does,
you're gonna get a sunburn.

My weeks went by looking forward to
and planning Friday night: selecting the bar for
cocktails, the restaurant for dinner, the variation on the uniform, and exchanging any late-
breaking information. Normally Kay, Max and
I would have at least three conference calls and
several e-mails to coordinate Friday night's activities, but for most of the spring we had a routine: cocktails at 7:30, dinner by nine, whatever
party by eleven, and home by two. But the routine wasn't ours alone—it always seemed like
the same several dozen or so faces in some ver-

sion of the uniform dancing, drinking, and flirting. The conversations were always short and superficial. "How are you? How's the gig? What's new? What are you drinking? Have you seen (someone from the party the week before)?" The fact that there was a whole subculture in the city that was doing the same things as I was took some of the burn out of being single again. *Everyone* was dancing, laughing, and scoping out the crowd.

You could usually count on there being at least one "admirer"—someone who looks good to you and vice versa, but does nothing more than watch you all night. After a few weeks at most the admirer might graduate to "Orbiter": One night he'll muster the courage to ask your name and dance with you. You'll even exchange numbers and e-mail addresses, but he won't contact you. But you'll see him again the next Friday night out, with a little more flirtation and a promise to call you during the week. "We should hang out," he'll say.

The pattern continues until you bump into him at a mutual friend's home, a cookout, a baby shower, a dinner party . . . You have a non-drunken-haze conversation and realize you actually *do* have more than the Friday night hangout in common. And he still doesn't call.

Mutual friends wonder out loud about why the two of you haven't hooked up yet. You find out he's been inquiring about your dating status. Friends say he's shy, slightly threatened by you, cautious and intrigued but afraid you'll blow him off. Like passing notes in elementary school, you plant the seed that if he calls and even perhaps asks you out you'll go. So maybe there's hope for making the orbiting admirer into a date. But no—during another Friday Night hangout, he'll dance with you, buy you a drink, you'll exchange numbers and e-mail addresses again; but he won't call you. Nor will he ever ask you out. That's because he's an Orbiter. Like Jules.

I'll always remember the first time I saw him. He was sitting at the end of the bar at the China Club watching the crowd, drinking a Bass Beer and sporting a Yankee baseball hat. He looked utterly content, as if he were watching a football game between teams he didn't care about. Kay was in a junior high school mood and dared me to "accidentally" bump into him. Like the simple friend of a junior high school girl, I took the dare and bumped into him. He laughed at me and shook his head. I guess someone had done that before. I felt like a gump, and did my best to become invisible very fast.

Of course, the next week, at the next party, he was there. Still embarrassed by my adolescent maneuver of the week before, I tried to avoid him. A couple of hours into the party I was resting my aching feet (I was wearing four-inch-heel boots and the deejay was playing old school hip-hop—a combination that can only be sustained for so long) when I looked up and saw Jules staring directly at me. I blushed and looked away. A half hour later we found ourselves standing next to each other at the bar. I smiled. He turned his back. I instantly wondered if I had some horrible rash no one had told me about, assuming I knew. When I finally reached the bar the bartender informed me that Mr. Back-turner had added me to his tab. I was slightly confused. But oh well. I tried to find him to say thanks, but he'd vanished.

Naturally he was there the *next* Friday. This probably sounds stupid, but I sort of liked the suspense of what each Friday might bring. While I was dancing with Max to Dr. Dre, Jules planted himself in the chair directly next to us. When the song finished and Biggie's "One More Chance" came on, he danced up behind me. I ignored him until mid-song but I didn't want to miss my chance to dance with him, and I knew Max would work it out. We danced four songs until the reggae came on, and I took my leave. He followed me.

"You've got Eveready Bunny energy."

"I'll take that as a compliment."

"It's meant to be. You hang out a lot? Seems like I see you every Friday."

"Well, all work and no play makes Jill a dull girl," I said, never being one to shy away from a cliché.

"And that makes you . . . Jill?"

I laughed and told him my name.

"I'm Jules. It's nice to finally meet you. Do you have a card? I'll give you a call sometime."

I smiled so hard you would have thought I'd hit the Lotto jackpot. Kay witnessed the episode. "So you got the digits." She gave me a high five. "Nice, very nice."

I was coming back down to earth. "Nuh-uh. He won't call. It's taken him three weeks to come up to me."

"If he were one of those trying-to-mack-you men, you'd be turned off. And now that he's not, you're all jaded. Give him a chance. See if he calls."

The week went by. No call. Friday night out again at Bar None, there he was. He greeted me with a kiss on the cheek and a very close hug like we were old prep school chums. Bought a round of drinks, danced with Kay and me, and when the night ended he said, "I'll give you a call this week." And so it went for the next three weeks: kiss on the cheek, very close hug, buys a round of drinks, dances with Kay and me, and ends the night with "I'll give you a call."

I was starting to think I was stuck in a buppie version of that Bill Murray movie *Groundhog Day*. Until the Friday night of the Fourth of July weekend. Jules appeared at the party, and I headed the other way. Enough was enough. I managed to avoid him most of the night, until Kay cornered me on the dance floor.

"Your boy is looking for you."

"Don't be ridiculous. Max knows where I am."

"Jules. He's been bugging me all night asking where you are."

Hand on my hip, "Please. What am I, his Friday night party partner?" He walked up behind me as the words came out of my mouth. Oops.

"Well, here you are. Are you avoiding me?"

I was busted, so I did the only self-respecting thing: I, um, euphemized. "No. No. I've just been flitting around. How are you?"

"Better now."

"Keep it."

He gave me a quizzical look. "Something I did? Something I said?"

"No, not really. But don't you find it just a *little* peculiar that every Friday we see each other, hang out, flirt, and then nada until the next week? It's like that movie *Groundhog Day*." Hah—only took me three weeks from the time I thought of it till I got the chance to bring it up "spontaneously."

"You mean, you actually thought I'd call you?"

"Well, duh—I gave you my card and it wasn't to pick chicken out of your teeth."

Either he was genuinely perplexed, or he was putting on a

good show of it. "But . . . I thought you gave your number to everyone. I mean, you're always out, you're always dancing with some guy, and it seems like you know half the crowd at every party. You never struck me as the kind of woman who'd want to go out on a *normal* date."

"A normal date!" I was floored. He thought I was just some party-dirty stay-out girl. I was insulted! "That's a hell of an assumption. And you know what they say about assuming—you make an ass out of you and me."

"Now I know."

"Now you do." Yeah, now he did, but he *still* didn't ask me out. I could feel steam rising from my head. I found Kay and told her I was ready to go.

"I'm sorry, but can you *believe* he said he didn't think I was the kind of woman that would go out on a date? Like I'm some *party*-girl?"

"I hate to break it to you, Ms. Mac, but you are rather flirtatious, and maybe even a little infamous."

My jaw dropped, but she gave me the Hold Up sign before I could say a word.

"Don't be mad 'cause he called it like he saw it. It's his loss if he can't appreciate a woman who enjoys going out and having a good time."

"Exactly. Now wait a second, Kay—do *you* think I'm over-exposed?"

She gave the ceiling a let's-see . . . look. "How long have you been on the guest list here? Who deejayed the last six parties? Who's deejaying the next one? Don't tell me—I already know you know the answers. Maybe you are a just a *bit* over-exposed."

So, great: not only was this guy never really interested in

me because he thought I was a party animal, but even one of my best friends agrees with him that I'm overexposed—and I don't even get any of the benefits of celebrity! My steam simmered to a slow burn, and finally a tepid sulk. I still had my resolution to go out every Friday night, but now I felt like I had to avoid my usual haunts, or at least give them a rest for a while. Well, okay, I thought, but what are my options? Am I supposed to go to clubs I don't like, with bad music and people who wouldn't like me any more than I would like them? What else: Singles cruise? Continuing ed? Charity work?

9

Good People

My Grandma always said . . .
You gotta know shit from Shinola.

The next week answered my question.
I was spending my precious Friday evening fill-
ing in for Olga at her mentoring program, trying to do my good deed for the month—both
for Olga and for her seven-year-old mentee,
Tisha. Tisha had seen a lot of the worst the
world can offer. Neglected and abused by parents who couldn't seem to stay sober, she had
bounced around in foster care since age three.
Tisha was one of the countless children in New
York City who needed positive adult interaction
that came not from "the system" but from a

place of generosity, caring, and hope. Olga had been Tisha's mentor for almost two years and almost never missed a session, but this evening she had a secret appointment she could not miss. So there I was in the community room of the Lincoln Houses on East One Hundred Thirty-fourth Street with about a dozen six-to-eight-year-olds and their mentors, all of us reading, drawing, painting, and playing games. Even though I griped when Olga asked me to take her place (and especially when she wouldn't tell me why), it was a welcome change of pace from cocktailing or surviving another date. Plus it gave me a week away from overexposure.

Tisha and I got to work cutting out magazine pictures for the collage we were creating. I liked the sounds of all the children playing, laughing, and creating. It was a safe space for them, and for me it felt like a mindful meditation, an escape from the workaday world's trials and tribulations. But my retreat was short-lived.

"Ms. Mac, I think Mr. Riley likes you. He keeps looking over here and smiling at us."

"Well, Tisha, boys do that sometimes, but it doesn't mean he 'likes' me. Maybe he's smiling just to smile."

"Unh-uh. Every time you look up he looks away. And he keeps bringing other paints and markers over here, and we already got enough stuff!"

Seven-year-olds can be so perceptive. But I was there to spend quality time and give back to the community, not meet my next date, so I paid him no mind. I mean, the nerve! There I was, trying to give a deprived child a few hours just to be a child, and some misguided "boy" was trying to get his flirt on. The last thing I needed right now was another man-boy who wasn't creative enough to figure out how to strike up a conversation. Besides, this was a community service activity, not a singles pick-up mixer. Tisha and I finished our collage, hung it on the wall, and headed for the pizza table.

"Uh, Ms. Mac and Ms. Tisha? Can Troy and I join you?"

Before I could say a word, little Ms. Tisha accepted for us. "Yes you can, but you have to sit between me and Ms. Mac." Troy sat on the other side, facing us.

Tisha tugged on my shirtsleeve. "See? I told you, Ms. Mac—he likes you!" Tisha my new chaperone, integrated Mr. Volunteer more smoothly than Olga had ever done with any of my wannabe suitors. That is, until she became the Littlest Inquisitor:

"What's your name?"

"Frank."

"You're Troy's new mentor, right?"

"That's right."

"You gonna stay?"

"I've committed to be here every Friday night for the next year."

"Where do you live?"

"Downtown. Thirty-eighth Street and Park Avenue."

Out of the corner of my eye I could see Troy trying to follow the conversation like it was a tennis match, his head bobbling back and forth as he watched the volley.

"Do you work?"

"Yes."

"What do you do?"

"I help companies find investors."

"You got a car?"

"Yes."

"What kind?"

"BMW."

"You got a wife?"

"No."

"Ever had a wife?"

"No."

"You got children?"

"No. But I have a niece and a nephew about your age."

"You got a girlfriend?"

"No."

"Why not?"

"Haven't met the right woman yet."

"You got friends?"

"Yes, ma'am." I could see he was trying very hard not to crack a smile, but she wasn't making it easy. "They're my frat brothers from college."

"Went to college, huh? What college did you go to?"

"Harvard."

"What are your friends' names?"

"Alex, James, and Dennis."

"They married?"

"Yes, all three of them."

"Hmmph." Tisha got up from the table to put the paper plates in the trashcan. I couldn't tell if she was satisfied with Frank's answers, and I could see from his bemused look that he didn't know, either. Olga had warned me that Ms. Tisha was a live wire, but what we'd just seen was only a warm-up. She returned to the table to tell Frank the real deal.

"See, Ms. Mac is substituting for my real mentor, Ms. Olga. They're best friends in real life. Ms. Mac, she doesn't have a boyfriend or a husband or nothing. She just works all the time. Now Ms. Olga, my real mentor, she has a husband, but he works late on Friday so she comes to see me so she won't be home by herself or out in the street with Ms. Mac and their other friends getting in trouble chasing men. But tonight Ms. Mac didn't want to get in trouble either, so she came to help me with my collage 'cause my real mentor, Ms. Olga, had an appointment."

Tisha was just too pleased with herself. I guess she felt she had told Frank all he needed to know. Her narrative of my life wasn't exactly what mine would have been, but I didn't hold it against her—kids tend to call it the way they see it, or just repeat it the way they've heard it. Of course, that meant Olga and I would have to have a few words . . .

Frank smiled at the story, though. "So Tisha, you think Ms. Mac would give me the time of day? Do you think she would call me if I gave her my number?"

"Well, I don't know. You may not be her type." She turned to me. "Ms. Mac, what's your type?"

I cleared my throat. "All right, guys. This is what would be known as an inappropriate conversation for little people. Mr. Riley, if you'd like to speak with me, perhaps you should do it *after*ward." He smiled, made a polite semi-bow, and took Troy back to their corner.

Tisha, on the other hand, wasn't quite the soul of subtlety. "So, so does that mean *he's* your type?" I gave her a look. "What? How come grown-ups never want to talk about good stuff around us kids?"

"Tisha!"

She squelched a yelp. "I'm sorry, Ms. Mac." Little contrite face. "Was I being sassy?"

"Yes, Tisha, that's a little over the top. Anyway, it's time for us to pack up and go home." I brought Tisha upstairs to her guardian, and headed out to the subway.

"Ms. Mac! Hey, Ms. Mac!"

I turned to see Frank trotting toward me.

"About inside—listen, I'm sorry. When I saw you come in you didn't strike me as the volunteering type. I was curious, but I didn't expect Tisha to go telling me all that stuff."

"Well, I guess she told you everything you needed to know." *Grrrr* . . .

"I don't know that I believed even half of it. Working all the time, maybe; not having a boyfriend, well, that'd make sense if you're working all the time, but . . ." He smiled.

"Okay, look, I *do* work a lot, and I *don't* have a boyfriend—but I don't chase men!"

He laughed, and I had to laugh with him. "Yeah, I—to tell the truth, I just couldn't picture it."

"Thank you."

"Oh, I didn't mean—Listen, are you heading downtown? I could give you a ride."

"You mean in your BMW?"

"Yeah, but it sounds more impressive than it is. It's only a 1999."

Actually, it looked, felt, and smelled brand new. As we drove along the East River on the FDR Drive, I learned a lot about him. For one thing, he volunteered as a way to give back to the community. He'd been raised in foster care himself in Brownsville, and with the love, care, and support of *his* after-school mentor, he was able to stay in school and excel— and ultimately get accepted to Harvard. But he didn't seem to think that proved he was anything special; in fact, almost the opposite: he fancied himself a modern-day Horatio Alger, and figured that if he could make it, anyone could.

"Young people just don't want to work for it. They want it all handed to them. The only thing they care about is what- ever the new whatever is—being hard, being in the thug life, being pimps and bitches and hoes, with fast money and fast cars." Any minute now I thought he was going to tell me how he was really a cranky seventy-year-old man who'd drunk a potion and switched bodies with a young brother. But no— and he had more to say.

"They don't want to be uncool. I was uncool all my life, but I was determined to make something out of myself. And it wasn't easy, especially when I got to Harvard. I didn't have half the stuff even most of the poor kids have now: no Nikes, no boom box. I got there the first day with a duffle bag and my determination. That's it: I couldn't even afford to have a slice of pizza off campus; if it wasn't on the meal plan, I was done. Oh, and forget about dating—once girls found out I was a foster kid from Brownsville, they tried to make me a charity case or ran as far from me as they could. It was like they were afraid my poverty would rub off on them somehow."

I almost said something, but it was obvious he was building up a head of steam, and I didn't want to get run over.

". . . I mean, these girls grew up in suburbia, went to whatever prep school, spent spring break on a beach and summer at the Vineyard. I had to work through every vacation because I didn't have a *home* to come back to, and didn't have a *mommy* or a *daddy* to put money in my *account*! I had to work *hard* and *save* to get where *I* am!" Now we were at the steering-wheel-banging phase.

"But *now*, now these same girls are calling and sweating me, trying to get me to spend two hundred dollars for dinner at some see-and-be-seen restaurant, like I'm supposed to spend my hard-earned dollars wooing them. Every time I get an award or there's an article about me, they invite me to their little parties, playing large like they care about people and issues and I'm good enough to hang out with them now because I've got means and position. But you know what? You want to know something? I'm not feeling *any* of that bourgeois crap. Yeah, so I have the Park Avenue penthouse and the country house in Greenwich, but they're *mine*. Those people can't do *anything* for me now."

I let the silence hang—well, the silence except for his breathing, which sounded like an old train engine huffing into the station. What could I have said? He clearly wouldn't be interested in any of *my* college stories—no matter how frustrated I got with my life sometimes, it could never qualify as hard. Frank's wounds were deep, and they weren't going anywhere anytime soon. I pulled out my cell phone as we got to Thirty-eighth Street.

"Well, thanks for the ride, Frank. I appreciate it."

"Whoa, hey, not so fast. How about a bite at Asia de Cuba? Cocktails at the Morgan Bar? I *still* don't know any more about you than what I got from Tisha."

"Yeah, well, that about sums it up. Anyhow, I've got to get up early in the morning." A taxi was pulling up just ahead of us, giving me my easy out. But did I take it? No. "Besides, you might think I was trying to get you to woo me, and we wouldn't want that. But thanks again for the ride."

"I didn't mean . . ." I could see the gears grinding as he tried to figure out what he *did* mean. "So can I call you?"

A couple got out of the cab, and I popped out of Frank's shiny BMW.

"I don't think so. Good night!"

As I stepped into the cab he yelled, "Yeah, I knew you were one of those good people! You ain't shit, either—like the rest of 'em! Fuck you!"

His face was tight with rage. For once in the bluest moon I

decided to let somebody else have the last word. I got in the cab, listening to his curses shrink to nothing as we drove away.

I dialed Bea as the cab headed toward the FDR Drive.

"Hey girl!" She answered on the first ring in her usual up-beat singsong. "What's doing? I was just about to call you."

"My sista, I'm doing. I'm on my way home."

"But it's Friday night—don't you have a date?"

"Well, Bea, let me tell you—"

"What happened now?" I could tell she was about to start some mundane task like painting her toenails.

"I went uptown to do some volunteer work tonight, only to have this guy who seemed like he might have dating potential try to pick me up after he insulted me."

"I'm confused. That doesn't even sound right. How could he insult you and then ask you out? You're leaving out some details, but okay, I'm listening . . ."

"Well, he was giving me a ride downtown—"

"Wait right there. You mean to tell me you got in a car with an absolute stranger? Have you lost all your good sense? I know you always have cab fare, and I know you learned not to talk to strangers, let alone not to get into strangers' cars. You better be glad you just had your sensibilities insulted and weren't assaulted. What's wrong with you?"

I hadn't even thought about that. Now I felt angry *and* stupid. "So anyway—"

"Anyway nothing!" Bea wasn't in a mood to cut me any slack. "I know you're in this take-back-the-night mode, but you better think and think again. You know what Mama used to say—Use your sixth sense, not just your book sense, because one plus one is two, but that won't tell you anything about how crazy people can be. Girl, that's my other line. I'll call you." She hung up.

Crossing the Brooklyn Bridge toward home, I realized that Bea was right. I had to be more careful—just because it shines doesn't mean it's not shit.

10

Making a Circle
into a Square

My Grandma always said . . .
Everything done in the dark
is gonna come to light

I met Van back when I was still with Luke, at the Black MBA conference in Detroit. He was there recruiting for his consulting firm, and my company's booth was next to his. We naturally gravitated toward each other; of course, it didn't hurt that he was a charming and funny, six foot two, soccer player who was lean and muscular, with expressive, almond-shaped chestnut-brown eyes.

During the slow periods in the booths we'd meet in the aisle and chat. Both of us were among the few people of color at our companies, and the only young people of color recruiting, and over three days at the conference we became pals. We'd meet for breakfast, scope out the companies with the best giveaways, meet for dinner, stay up late talking about everything under the sun—work, sports, family, relationships, community building, novels, and music—and generally just have fun.

He was a small town boy from Alabama, but otherwise my type of well-rounded guy. He went to work, loved his family, especially his mother and father, went to church on Sundays, and played on his firm's softball team. He seemed to live a stable, no-drama life, and he was just plain nice. At the end of the conference, we exchanged cards and promised to look each other up whenever we might be in the other's city—although it was obvious he'd likely be in New York before I'd ever be in Alabama. It was a rare pleasant encounter without the bullshit promise to keep in touch.

One Friday afternoon I got a call. "Hi. This is Van. I don't know if you remember me, but we met some time ago at the Black MBA Conference. How are you?"

"I'm well, thanks, and I do remember you. What have you been up to?"

"Well, I moved to New York about three months ago. The company's New York office needed another associate and my girl and I broke up, so I figured it was my chance to give the big city a whirl."

"I'm sorry to hear about you and your girlfriend. I guess it must be something in the water."

"You recently broke up too?" He sounded almost excited, which gave me a twinge of worry that he might be another Marauder, with an open wound from the last committed relationship that he wants to fill with the next one—NOW. Still, I didn't want to be rude . . .

"It's been a while, but yeah. Dating in the city takes its toll."

"I know what you mean. These last few months have definitely been . . . odd."

"Really? How so?"

"Well, why don't we meet for dinner and I'll tell you all about it. Are you free tonight?"

I hated to admit it, but my big plan for the evening was watching *Law & Order: Special Victims Unit* and ordering in Keur N' Deye (best Senegalese food outside of Senegal)—or at best convincing Kay or Max to meet for a snack in the neighborhood. "As a matter of fact, tonight is a good night. I should be out of work by 7:00 P.M."

"Great! You're the New Yorker, where should me meet?"

"Pick a part of town. Do you have a taste for anything in particular?"

"I do, but they don't make it in restaurants."

"Excuse me?"

"I was just thinking nothing beats home cooking, but I love Italian. Anyplace you like? I haven't been out much since I moved to New York, so . . ."

"Then let's go to Monte's on LaGuardia and Bleecker. It has some of the best Italian in the city, even if the décor leaves something to be desired."

"Cool. 8:00 P.M. work for you?"

"Sure."

"I'll see you then."

Great! I caught my reflection in the computer screen. Oh, no—*not* great. This was not one of my better fashion days. I'd woken up late and tossed on khakis, a white cotton button-down shirt, and loafers. I looked preppy, and not in a good way. I redid the bun and put on some makeup. This was as good as it was going to get today. And I reminded myself that if he didn't dig me busted, he wouldn't dig me spit-shined and polished. Besides, he was new to the city and hopefully hadn't been indoctrinated into the city dating culture. He'd seemed grounded, focused, and stable when I met him. He hadn't struck me as needing to sow his oats. Even if it didn't work out, he could be someone new to hang out with.

I was on time and so was he. We walked in together giving each other the do-I-know-you? look. He looked just the way I remembered him: Fine.

"Van?"

"Hey!" He gave me a bear hug like I was a long-lost relative who would be leaving him an inheritance. Dinner was pleasant. We talked about all the same things we'd talked about in Detroit—work, sports, family, relationships, community building, novels, music—and his move to New York. Moving to the city without any specific affinity group from college, grad school, friends, family, or a significant other can be rather challenging. He'd gone to college and law school in Alabama and had stayed close to home until now. Since moving, he hadn't been very social, he *said*—but he knew all the new spots and which were the good nights. This kind of information is not available in *Time Out*—you'd have to go and hang out to know.

"It's still early—you want to check out the Exchange Club? Ever been there?"

I was having a pleasant time, so I figured *why not?* "Sure. I've been there a few times." And off we went. Arriving at the Exchange Club, Walt, one of the Orbiters, was at the door and greeted me with hugs and kisses, letting us in without charging the cover.

Van chuckled. "Hey, for someone who's only been here a few times, you're pretty well known."

"I'm a little social." Just as I was about to suggest heading toward the bar, a woman in a hot pink glitter-coated halter dress that didn't cover too much above the waist besides her nipples, sashayed over to Van.

She spoke in a breathy bimbo voice that matched her look exactly. "Long time, no see, Van. Where've you been hiding?"

"Oh, I've just been working."

"But you didn't call me back. Didn't you have a good time the other weekend?" She let out a giggle.

"Umm, let me introduce you to a friend."

She looked me up and down, and rolled her eyes. "Is *that* why you didn't call me back?" I quickly upgraded her from breathy bimbo to irate ho. "Is *she* one of your little hometown girls?"

I'd stumbled into some mess. She was looking for a scene, and I wasn't in the mood for any cattiness, especially over Van. "Excuse me. I'll be back." Girlfriend should have had some dignity and not assumed. If he doesn't call you back and you see him in the street, say hi and strut on, and tell yourself it's his loss. But girlfriend wasn't exactly looking for my advice. I walked away and bumped into Pia, one of Max's ex-flings.

"Hey, how are you? I saw you walk in. Are you with Van?"

"Nn-not exactly. You know him?"

"Yeah, I met him a few months ago. Nice work if you can get it, if you know what I mean."

"No—what *do* you mean?"

"Girlfriend, he is packing, and he has skills. I wouldn't date him, but he'd make an excellent stash for the dry spells."

"Van? But he just got here. He seems like a nice country boy."

"Chile, be real—that's his *game*. Oh, here comes Nature Boy now."

Van walked up. "I see you guys know each other. I guess New York is a small town after all. Can I buy you ladies a drink?"

"Smaller than you think," Pia smiled. "I'm drinking Grey Goose on the rocks."

"I'll have Ketel One and tonic."

Van looked startled. At first I thought it was our drink order but then I saw another sista rushing toward him from across the room. She was toothpick-thin, in a black cat suit, with dyed blond shoulder-length bone-straight hair. She was also madder than a wet hen, and her head and index finger were about to start wagging.

"I *knew* I'd see you here. I thought you were a nice wholesome man. You're just like all the rest, a hoe and a player. Playing like you all *dignified*—shoot, I *saw* you coming out of the St. Regis the other night with that nasty Thea. I bet you fucked her, too! I hope you wore a glove, because she's a burner!"

She looked like she might swing at him. Pia and I looked at each other and headed toward the bar, leaving Van to take his beat down.

Pia started to laugh. "That brother better learn some dick control or he's not going to have one. And he'd *better* learn to leave the psychos and the wild ones alone, or they're gonna have all his business in the street."

"Well, I guess he's in a little over his head. I think he just discovered he's not in Kansas anymore." Damn—and here I thought he might have some possibility.

Van reappeared at the bar, looking browbeaten but trying to put a good face on it.

"So, uh, how about that drink now?"

"Looks like *you* need one," said Pia, "but I'll pass. It's pumpkin time for me." And she was off.

"So much for your choirboy image, Van. I can see you've been getting around."

"I know it looks bad, but that was just one of those things. She's looking for something I can't give."

I didn't take the bait. It was more than I wanted to know. I sipped my drink, bopped my head to the tunes, and thought about how to make a graceful exit. Mr. New-to-New-York wasn't so fine anymore, and he *did* have high drama.

Van broke the silence. "So what else do people do in the city on the weekends, other than hang out at places like this?"

"Depends upon what you're into. Everyone has things they like to do, and they tend to find others who like to do the same things. For some it's the gym, church group, arts and craft classes, book clubs, or spending time with friends. I think folks find other like-minded people."

"Coming from a place where everyone knows everyone, it's been some time since I had to make friends. I've been out some, but mostly with people from the office, and I really want to keep my personal life separate from my professional life. I go to the gym to work out, not chat; I go to church to worship, and that's that. So . . . so how have you managed to keep your sanity in the city?"

"You know, I don't know. I hadn't thought about it. I don't have any family here, but I do have friends—from prep school, college, grad school, previous jobs, classes I've taken. I've always been rather social and chatty, so I just meet people." What I didn't say was *too bad I can't seem to meet a man I'd trust with my laundry.*

"Like when you met me, and the guy at the door?"

"I guess. I'll chat up damn near anyone. I believe that everyone has something to offer." *Including you—and clearly you feel you have to offer it to the sleaziest women you can find.*

"So what do you think I have to offer?"

"Quite honestly," *she said, lying,* "I don't know. I haven't thought about it."

"Well?"

"Well . . ." *Oh, go ahead—tell him the truth.* "If tonight's any indication, I'd say what you have to offer is trouble."

He laughed. "The kind your boyfriend might want you to avoid, right?"

"You're assuming I have one."

"Oh, I know you said you broke up a while ago, but you mean to tell me a sista like you is single in New York?"

That's a good move—make me feel defensive. "There's nothing wrong with that. There's a whole bunch just like me—single, dignified, *and* happy."

"Well, then you sistas need to come to Alabama. The women there are interested in getting married, having children, and being settled—period. They are *not* interested in having fun, or enjoying life."

"And what makes you think women here don't want the same thing?"

"For one thing, you all have other interests. You're not so man-centered, or relationship-centered. You all seem to care less about it. You don't cook or make pies. You have schedules and calendars, busy, busy, busy. Are you in a relationship right now?"

"Oh, no."

"See? You say it like it's a disease—like you don't *want* to be in one."

"I'm not averse to a relationship, but I'm still figuring out who I am and what I want. And I hate to burst your bubble, but most women—urban, suburban, small-town—whether they admit it or not, want someone in their lives and they *do* want fun. What they *don't* want is drama." You don't want to get me going like this, when I think I'm the spokesperson for Women of the World. But . . . "If a woman likes a man well enough, and he treats her the way she wants to be treated, cooking *might* transpire. But many of us have learned the hard way that few men are worthy of the time and effort cooking requires. For the busy woman, cooking is special."

"Uh-huh." He was nodding his head like he agreed with me so far. "And so what do you do for sex?"

"Um, well, we work it out as needed."

"I didn't mean *all* women, I meant *you*—when's the last time *you* worked it out, as needed?"

"Don't you think that's a little personal?"

"It's just between us girls. I'm just curious and you're deflecting my question."

"You sure you can handle the truth?"

"I'm a big boy."

So I heard—it's a shame you're not a grown man. But what the hell . . . "Last week—last Friday to be exact."

He blushed. "So you *are* seeing someone."

"No that just means I have someone I work it out with. That's all."

"I see. Was it good?"

"I don't kiss and tell. And here you almost had me fooled into believing you were a nice, clean-cut young man."

"I am, but like any nice, clean-cut young man, a pretty woman causes my nature to rise." He smiled, and I suddenly felt like little Red Riding-Hood visiting the wolf.

"I'd sure hate to do that to you."

"You wouldn't help out a poor single lonesome brother new to New York with a little old-fashioned hospitality?"

Oh, that's it. "It seems you've already had plenty of New York hospitality, and you surely don't need mine. But if you still need more, you can find the kind you're looking for on Tenth Avenue after dark. Van, thanks for dinner, but I've got to go."

"Oh come on—you're lot of fun. After a few more cocktails, you might change your mind."

What I thought was *So was it your momma or your daddy who taught you to tell a woman you want to get her drunk enough to go to bed with you against her better judgment?* What I said was, "Sorry, but I don't get down like that. I don't know you, and I don't think I want to." I left Van standing at the bar. I was sure he would find some chick in the Exchange Club who was more than willing to provide "a little old-fashioned hospitality," but it wasn't going to be me. In the cab home I had to laugh at myself. Maybe watching *Law & Order: Special Victims Unit* and ordering in Keur N' Deye on a Friday night wasn't so bad after all.

11

Renegers:

Running a Boston

My Grandma always said . . .
You ain't got to tell it all.

Having been in the game for a while, I'd honed my skills enough to be able to spot the telltale signs of the reneger. Vanity (the deadly sin, not Prince's 1980s protégée) and arrogance are easy giveaways.

Max called. "Go out last night?"

"Sort of."

"What happened?"

"Well, Vincent and I were supposed to go to dinner and a movie, but he was nearly two hours late. He kept calling every thirty minutes saying he was getting dressed, giving me a play-by-play of his wardrobe dilemmas, and asking my advice. It was just weird. Finally he showed up all shined, shaven, and smelling good, but all that to just wear jeans and a T-shirt!"

Max laughed. "Come on, now."

"I'm serious! Don't get me wrong—I always appreciate a well-groomed man, but two hours? And it was all low-budget from there on in. We missed the movie but made our dinner reservations. Then all through dinner he kept saying, 'You know I'm self-absorbed?' It was not a rhetorical question. I got it the first time. I had to ask him what his point was. *What else are you telling me?* I couldn't tell if it was insecurity, fear, poor social skills, or another case of a brother with Tourette's syndrome. No shit Sherlock—it took him two hours to get dressed and put on jeans. I got that he was self-absorbed or just plain old narcissistic. Whatever the reason, I'm not playing. Six times during the course of one dinner was just too much for me. People always tell you everything you need to know and if you're listening you can spare yourself some drama. I passed on dessert and was ready to head home."

"Now that's a lot. I'm sorry."

"Wait, there's more—check this out. On the way home he says, 'So what *else* do you like to do, besides dinner and movies?' Being the scintillating conversationalist I am, I say, 'Well, pool and bowling are fun.' I don't know why I said that, but they were the first things that came to my mind. But then *he* says, 'Pool and bowling? That's what average people do.' So *I* ask him, 'Oh, well what do *special* people do—shuttle back and forth between the ballet and the opera?' And do you know what this man said?"

Max was laughing hard. "Go ahead, tell me."

"He looked me deep in the eyes, and said—and I'm not

making this up—'You need to learn to surrender. You need to surrender to me, to submit yourself. Let go. Let me be the man.' This fool had watched *An Officer and a Gentleman* one time too many. The only surrendering I'm doing is to God and French fries, and he *clearly* wasn't either. I couldn't get out of the car fast enough."

"You're hard on a brother. Cut him some slack. Not everyone is going to dig your ways of being."

"Well if I'm the prize . . ."

"Yeah, he's a stupid fool. But you gotta be a *little* more flexible."

"So you're saying I'm rigid?"

"No, but I'm saying this is not work. You don't have to *surrender*, but sometimes you've got to relax and let things flow. Let the guy take the lead. That's what's wrong with you modern woman professional-types. You always gotta be in control."

I don't know if he was *trying* to get me riled up, but he was doing a great job. "Oh, you're so full of shit! I guess you think I should do the 'whatever-you-want-baby' routine. Or maybe I should quit my gig and become a helpless, no-drive, no-ambition, checkout-counter girl?" I put on the breathless bimbo voice I'd heard from Van's little friend: 'Oh baby! You're so big and strong, and I'm so lost and helpless. I just need you to take care of me!' "

Max snorted. "Hey, you sound cute like that. See, if you'd talk to *me* that way, maybe we'd be able to get together."

"Max, you're really tripping now. You wouldn't know what to do with me if you could have me."

He laughed. "Wanna try me?"

"Shut up. And anyway if I were a stripper or a checkout

girl, you men would be saying, 'oh, chickenhead, gold digger, trying to get my stuff, blah blah blah . . .' You *all* need to get a grip, join the new century and figure out what you want, 'cause you *can't* have it all."

"Well, the stripper thing doesn't sound too bad—but I wouldn't marry her."

"See? That's exactly what I'm talking about. Men try to do a head game on women all the time. If by some whack twist of fate a sista doesn't get an education and has to hustle to make ends meet, doing the best she can, and placates and exploits the fragile male ego to get what she wants, then all she can be is somebody's baby's mama. *But,* if a sistar figures out how to get an education, get a job, build a career, or do a few things for herself, oh, she's trying to be in control and no man can do anything for her."

"Aw, now . . ."

"Don't you 'aw, now' me!" *Note to men: you should* never *'aw, now . . .' a woman when she's diagnosing all the ills of the male gender.* "The truth is, everyone wants someone who they can rely on, who makes them feel special, needed, and cared for. It doesn't matter who they are or what they do."

"Easy, playa! So I guess you'll be going out with the old boy again?"

"Oh, hell no!"

"Well, good. He sounds weak to me, and you need a solid brother. What are you doing next Friday night?"

"What, you mean *besides* plotting how to control and verbally castrate some men? Wait—are you asking me out?"

"Silly ass—come with me to my boss's card party. You can play bid whist but you'd better show and prove. Don't embarrass me."

"What kind of invitation is that?"

"One where Frazier, the colleague you keep sweating me about, is going to be there."

"Ohhh . . ."

So Friday night we headed to Connecticut to play bid whist at Max's boss's house. I'd met Doug a couple of times, once when I took Max his spare keys to the office, and once at Max's thirtieth birthday party. Doug lived the good life. He'd worked on the Street since business school, been fast-tracked and then became the firm's youngest CEO. He, his trophy wife, and picture-perfect children lived on a ten-acre estate in Greenwich. Twice a year he held card parties for his clients, friends, and star protégés. Max and Frazier were the stars of the moment, having closed ten deals in three months.

By the time we arrived, the veteran bid whist players and Frazier were at the table. The first hand was underway, with all the customary shit-talking that bid whist requires. Frazier was taking a verbal jousting from Doug's mentor, Judge Davis. The judge was the elder statesman, about seventy, gruff, loud, and very toasted.

"You the last bid, boy. What you bidding? You don't need no algebraic formula to figure out what you got in your hand," the judge chided. "They didn't teach you nothing 'bout this at—where'd you go to business school, boy?"

Frazier, expressionless, replied flatly. "Harvard, Judge."

"Bam!" the judge shouted, smacking a jack of spades as the lead card down on the table. He was definitely drunk, but he might also have had a hot hand. He and his partner had bid seven. Everyone played relatively quietly, except the judge, who said with each hand he won (which was all of them), "Well now, black people. This is how you get to the top." And to Max: "You better head on back up there—where'd you say you went to school now? Was that Boston?" He made himself laugh. He'd "Run a Boston" on the young cats.

Frazier was out of his league and shouldn't even have sat down at the table. The next hand he bid board, meaning he didn't have a winning hand. The game continued, and when his turn came, he reneged.

Now reneging is the act of *not* playing the suit that's on the table when it's in your hand. You get caught reneging when someone at the table remembers that you said you *didn't* have a particular suit when it comes up again. I was standing behind Frazier, looking over his shoulder and watched him do it. Judge Davis was merciless.

"Boy, now I know you said you went to Harvard and all, but a heart is a heart. You cut it last time with a spade just to prevent me from making ya'll head up to the home of the tea party. They taught you that at Harvard now. Your sorry card-playing behind—just get up from the table. You're done." The judge kept muttering as Frazier left the table and headed for the bar.

Anyone who reneges at a table filled with veterans is either too cocky or too stupid to think he won't be found out and made to lose face. Not only will you be clowned, but no one will want to partner with you for a long time. Renegers never fully live it down, especially when they've claimed they can play, or talked a lot of shit while playing. I should have read the tea leaves—or the cards for that matter.

After embarrassing himself, I guess Frazier knew it was time to leave and avoid further humiliation by the judge. "Are you heading back to the city? I'll give you a ride back if you can stand being in the same car with a Reneger." He shook his head and laughed. "I don't know what I was thinking." Max was staying at Doug's for the weekend to brown nose, so I said yes, but on the ride home I couldn't resist needling him.

"Did you think all that Knob Creek the judge was drinking blurred his senses? You *know* that man has been playing bid whist longer than both of us combined have been alive."

"You can't blame a man for trying." Frazier laughed, a nice, easy laugh. All right, so he reneged, but at least he could laugh at himself.

I couldn't believe that Max had finally hooked a sista up. Frazier was funny, flirtatious, and fine. He was also full of himself, enough to "invite" *me* to cook *him* dinner the following Friday.

"Max says you can burn, so what do you say about practicing your skills on *me*? I eat out most of the time, and I do appreciate home cooking. And you know what they say about the way to a man's heart." Normally I would have balked at that kind of presumption, but since Max had created the opportunity, I felt obliged to accept. *Note to self: Don't do that anymore.*

Why? To begin with, on Friday night he showed up empty-handed, a clear sign of no home training. You *always* take something when you go to someone's house for dinner. He didn't even think to bring a bottle of ginger ale from the corner store.

Then, while I set the table, he busied himself criticizing my living room furnishings.

"I have to say, I gave you credit for having more imagination. I mean, your living room looks like it's straight out of Crate & Barrel—or maybe Pottery Barn. It is kind of earthy and comfortable in here, though, I'll give you that."

Was that supposed to be a compliment?

But he was just warming up. He went on to critique my art-work (too black—I should consider more modern art); my music (I had the beginnings of a decent jazz collection, but it was "shallow" and my hip-hop choices were "obvious"), and my books (too eclectic but no crime novels). In the kitchen I steadied myself and decided I'd just listen for now. I began tab-ulating the insults and waiting for my moment to silence him for good.

"I'm famished! You about done in there?"

I turned on my best Martha Stewart cheer. "As a matter of fact I am."

Before I could put my napkin in my lap, he had attacked the table like ants at a picnic. He also managed to attack me while he was at it. "You were tasting while you were cooking." "You should watch your carbs—summer's coming." "The spinach could use some more garlic." "Probably should have taken the chicken out a couple of minutes sooner, and it really needs black pepper."

I could hear my heart beating in my head, but I held on. "Anything else? How about the potatoes?"

"Mm, now that you mention it, too much salt."

The serving bowls were empty and his plate clean. There wasn't a morsel in sight.

In my Martha Stewart voice once again: "Well, I'm so glad you enjoyed dinner." It took all my strength to resist rolling my eyes.

He didn't even offer to help clear the table, load the dish-washer, or anything. He just pushed back in the chair and mas-saged his now extended gut. "So what's your deal? You don't have a man, and baby, I got needs."

"Well, *baby*, I'm a woman and I got needs, too. And right now, I *need* you to get the *fuck* out of my house."

He said I was snooty. He said I was spoiled. He said I was selfish. He said I was self-absorbed. He said I was difficult. He said I was evil. And, just when I was afraid he might have missed something, he said I wasn't all that, anyway.

I said nothing. I just opened the door and showed him out. It was disappointing, but I should have known; bid whist reveals a lot. After all, he was a Reneger.

12

The Dating Food Chain

My Grandma always said . . .
You better situate yourself.

After all this dating with no Prince Charming in sight or even on the horizon, I had to access myself and try to make some sense of all the shenanigans. The guys I had gone out with did not know each other, but they all knew me. The more I thought about it, the more I realized that I'd been approaching dating all wrong. I hadn't been dating with any clear goals in mind, beyond my first goal of going out every week to get myself past Mr. Greenjeans.

With a few exceptions, I'd pretty much accepted whoever or whatever had shown up and expressed even the faintest interest in me. I was like a drowning person grabbing at anything that moved. No wonder I was always finding myself in situations that ended with drama, disgust, or plain old disappointment. But was I *really* expecting too much? I never wanted to be one of those women with a checklist: He must be/own/have done *x*, *y* and *z*. But after having to throw so many back into the sea, it hit me that my head and my heart must not be in sync; I just had no idea what it would take to get them together. So I called my uncle. Sixty years old, divorced twice, married three times—he *had* to have some insight into the male of the species.

"Uncle, got a minute?"

"For you, maybe even an hour. What's up? Got a new boyfriend yet?"

"Well, that's what I was calling about. I think I'm officially confused."

"Confused?" He laughed. "You're not confused, you're just beginning to get clear, that's all. But what is it you *think* you're confused about?"

"Men. At this age I thought I'd figured out a few things, but the more I do this dating thing the more it feels like I'm having a second adolescence. It all just seems like I'm a fish trying to swim on land."

"Love, I hate to break it to you, but you probably are. Clearly most things about living and life we don't learn in school. You know as well as anyone that the things we *most* need to understand are the things we're taught the *least* about; men and women dealing with each other sure is at the top of that list. But what *specifically* do you think is the problem?"

"Well, I want to say it's *me*. I just don't understand how to deal with men anymore—if I ever did. It's like there's always an agenda that I didn't get the memo about."

"Look, I can tell you a few things you're not gonna like or even want to hear, but it's the real deal. You want it?"

I could tell he was really serious because he started talking real country. Suddenly I got scared. "Um, since you put it that way, I don't know . . ."

"Now, you called me. If you want more nonsense, then keep doing it your way. But you see it's not working. It's like the Holland Tunnel is closed but you keep trying to go through. Maybe there's another way to get to New Jersey."

"Okay, now I'm really confused, but go ahead. I'm listening."

"Good—you see, you and a lot of others your age don't get that there are gradations between dating and marriage. And if you don't know that, and you're careless or unclear, you could find yourself stuck like a car with a flat tire on a dark country road without a spare tire, a cell phone or AAA."

I should have asked him for the no-metaphors version, but it was too late for me to be choosy.

"I'm gonna keep it real, like you young people say. Here it is: Figure out early on if you gonna make someone a fuck buddy, someone to do things with, your significant other, or the one you gonna marry. *You* get to determine who and what it's gonna be, and here's why: Women run the show. Problem is, most of the time y'all don't realize it 'cause you're planning out that knight-in-shining-armor nonsense or looking for Mr. Perfect when none of us is even close. Everybody got faults and flaws, and you got to figure out what you can deal with and what you can't. You got to know what's important to you, 'cause *you* got to deal with them. And most important, you better know who you are and what you're up to."

I swallowed hard. "Wow. That was a lot more truth than I was expecting."

"Good. Now be quiet, 'cause I ain't through yet. Now a relationship with a fuck buddy is purely transactional. It's just pure sinful lust. You know that's one of the deadly sins but be sure you're up for the consequences and don't get it confused. You're not going to the movies with your fuck buddy, or bringing him to hang out with your friends. He isn't coming to meet your mama, and you ain't coming to meet his. He shows up and you get it on, no attachment, wham, bam, thank you, ma'am. Women and men both confuse sex, intimacy, and love all the time. Unfortunately, many men can have sex with someone and it doesn't mean a thing—they might as well have had a sandwich. It's emotionally immature but you already know they're out there. You're grown, so you're gonna do what you're gonna do. Just be sure that's what you want, and understand that's *all* it is. Don't think it'll change one day. How you start with a fuck buddy is how it is."

"Uncle, that's ugly."

"I told you. But that's not all. You can find a man to be someone you do things with—like y'all say, 'hanging out.' That's someone who is just your friend. You go to movies, maybe dinner, maybe a party or a game, but you're friends, and you don't cross the proverbial line. That way you have room to see what the deal is. Maybe you think he's a nice person, not really your type, but good company. And at the end of the day that's what really matters. Friends tend to outlive lovers anyway, and given that you don't really know what you want yet in a spouse, having a whole lot of somebodies you can do things with is a good idea. Group outings—I know that sounds like a thing of the past, but if you and your single female friends tried it sometime, y'all might meet a decent man of some substance and have less nonsense. Either way, socializing when it's not 'a date' helps you get a sense of what you like and don't like. Besides, in this day and age there's too much stuff going around that penicillin won't fix. Folks need to be friends before they're anything else; then you can know if a guy's someone you want to be your 'man friend.' *Then* if y'all decide to date you got fewer surprises and a whole lot less drama. You know each other a little bit; you can behave like mature adults. You've created the basis for a 'real' relationship—like communication, negotiation, understanding likes and dislikes. Then you can decide for yourself what you're up to and play in the possibility of what you two can create together, what you're willing to give. Otherwise you're not gonna get very much if you're always trying to get something from the other person."

"Well, that's very—"

"Yeah, I know it sounds like one of those self-help books but it's true. You have to be able to share your thoughts and feelings, be vulnerable, and discuss things. Folks have to figure out how to discuss expectations. Otherwise, it'll end up in an upset and then it's too late. Folks got to be at least in the same boat if they're trying to reach the shore. One can't be swimming in the sea and the other rowing the boat."

"Does my aunt know about this?"

"Smarty-pants, how do you think we've stayed married for the last fifteen years? I haven't been married three times for nothing. I made more than my share of mistakes, and I still do, but I have learned a few things along the way. We all have a process we have to go through to figure out the difference between being in love and loving someone. And another thing: Don't get blinded by your desire to "be" with someone. If he hangs out all the time with his boys, don't think 'cause you get together that's gonna stop. Maybe for a while but not permanent. Folks can pretend usually for about three to six months and then the truth is gonna show up. You can't change or save anybody. You can choose to do things differently but your core is going to remain the same. How you meet them is how you get them. If they are smoking dope when you meet them, they're gonna keep smoking dope and will stop only because *they* decide for themselves that's something they don't want to do anymore. When you meet him and he got another woman, he gonna keep that other woman until he decides he don't want her or she puts him down. Most likely she's gonna have to put him down, otherwise he'll play both ends to middle until he can't play anymore. You can make yourself crazy trying to re-create yourself, thinking that'll make him want you more, but *you* decide whether you're gonna participate in the madness. The best thing is just to move on."

He stopped talking for a moment, and I was afraid he somehow figured out that I'd been doodling ornate question marks the whole time he was talking. Luckily, he was just catching his breath.

"On the other hand, don't believe that every man has another woman stuck somewhere. Folks may make a mistake from time to time and that's just because the flesh is weak and folks aren't focusing on what's important; they're not willing to have the conversation about what's really going on. It's an immature way—acting out. If the divorce is not final when you meet him and he's really interested in you, he'll show back up after the final decree. People who are truly interested in you aren't going to try to put you in the middle of their mess. But *remember*—*you* decide what you're gonna deal with and accept; you have to give an account for what you do and don't do. You can't make someone else pay his piper. You can only pay yours. You dig?"

"I hear you."

"Listen, I know that's probably not what you wanted to hear, but I'm not one to feed you that 'you're perfect and they're all dogs' nonsense. You're not, and they're not. You just got to get clear and figure out what you're gonna do and with whom. He'll show up when you stop bullshittin' yourself and go situate yourself. All right, beautiful?"

Well that wasn't what I wanted to hear but I got the point. It was time for me to go situate myself.

"God don't like ugly and

ain't crazy about beauty"

13

Barbie Wanted— But I'm Skipper!

My Grandma always said . . .
You better work all your assets

Olga calling Thursday evening:
"What are you doing tomorrow night?"

"Getting my hair done. Why?"

"Come go with me to this record-release party. Claude's going to be out of town and I'm not trying to roll solo. I might find trouble."

"You, Ms. Happily Married? I thought your trouble-finding days were long gone."

"Mm, well, I don't know . . ."

I've known Olga a long time—long enough to know that "Mm, well, I don't know . . ." does *not* mean "I don't want to talk about it."

It means, "Just ask me once more and I'll open the flood-gates." Unfortunately, it also means, "And I'm not asking for any feedback." Watch.

ME: "What's that supposed to mean?"

OLGA: "You know, I'm beginning to wonder why I got married. We never see each other, we don't have real conversations anymore, we're like ships passing in the night. Half the time he's out of town, and when he's *in* town the *last* thing he wants to do is spend time with me: He's either asleep, at the gym, or watching a game. And then he has the nerve to come to bed and want some ass! I am not feeling the love right now."

ME: "I had no I—"

OLGA: "I even suggested scheduling a date night to spend some quality time together, and all he did was shrug his shoulders! Most attention I've gotten in months was last week at the Project S.H.E. Gala. He was all but ignoring me—anything I said he just rolled his eyes and mumbled, like I was his ugly cousin and somebody forced him to take me to the prom—*until* some little old man started flirting with me. All of a sudden we were joined at the hip. I could barely go to bathroom—I think he even waited outside the door. I keep asking myself what it could be, 'cause I'm not gonna find out from him. Like, was it the new dining room furniture? I asked him about it, and he didn't say anything, so I ordered it and had it delivered. It wasn't cheap, but we're both doing well and now we can finally have a proper dinner party. Is it my weight? I've picked up a few pounds since the wedding, but I'm still fitting into a size 6. When he's in town I do my best to be home at a decent hour, but he knows what I do, and when I *can't* be home I always invite him to all the events that

I have to go to; and he *always* declines. And even when I make one of the junior people go in my place so I can come home and make dinner, he either says he's not hungry, or he eats but barely says ten words."

ME: "Olga, that's really—"

OLGA: "Oh, it's probably just a phase newlyweds go through. It's probably nothing. But anyway, are you coming with me?"

ME: "Um, sure. Sure. There's nothing worse than being all hair did and having nowhere to go. What time should I be ready?"

OLGA: "Let's say 9:30, and we'll be there by ten. I'll show my face and we can be home by midnight."

When Olga's colleague Kurt met us at the door of S.O.B.'s (Sounds of Brazil, but nobody calls it that), the opening band had just finished and the place was packed. Olga had told me in advance that Kurt was striking but not my type. Razor thin, lanky, with a protruding Adam's apple, he'd pass for a black Ichabod Crane if he didn't have a square jawline and chiseled features. We made our way towards the front where we joined Olga's assistant and another woman whose face was so familiar, though I couldn't remember where I knew her from. As we settled in, Kurt introduced her. She was the model on the cover of last month's *Glamour*. Throughout the evening Olga and I tried to chat her up, but she either wouldn't or couldn't say very much, especially if Kurt was at the table. From what we could tell, she was a very sweet woman who just happened to be drop-dead gorgeous, and figured out how to make a living from it. Kurt and Olga spent most of the night talking shop, and I just enjoyed the music, glad not to be sitting at home.

The next morning Olga called me ridiculously early.

"Olga, this better be critical. It's 8:30 on a Saturday morning. A.M."

"Okay, what did you say to Kurt last night?"

"Timeout—8:30 A.M. on a Saturday, *and* I'm getting the Inquisition?"

"He called me fifteen minutes ago, asking about you."

"Oh, yeah? So what did you tell him?"

"It was all positive, but I tried to curb his enthusiasm. Girl, he's cool to work with and hang out with, but I'd never fix him up with any of my friends. And given that you are my friend, that includes you."

"Why, what's his deal?"

"He loves beautiful woman—I'm not saying you're not, but you're not the downtown model beautiful."

"Oh—I got it."

"Yeah and he doesn't have the nicest reputation for how he treats them either. He had some woman show up at the office, curse him out in French, throw a bag of cut up clothes at him, and threaten to have his legs broken. Serious high drama and not good for office PR. Are you peeing?"

"Go ahead. You have my undivided attention." *Well, mostly.*

"But of course he's a boy so he can get away with that type of nonsense, proving his manhood by his arm candy—and they're always either the super-young are-you-sure-she's-legal type, or the overripe *Playboy/Penthouse* bombshell type. The rest of the boys in the office worship his simple ass because he's always surrounded by a bevy of beauties. And he's *not* a fan of chocolate—I don't think he likes his mama much. I've only seen him with one sista since we've worked together, and I have to say she *was* all that *and* a bag of chips, but she wasn't around very long; none of them ever are. And then he's always got a new babe while the old one's trail is still warm."

"That's great, Olga. Now *why* are we talking about this fool, let alone at . . . 8:42 A.M.?"

"Because here he is calling *me* this morning before a civilized hour, with some nonsense that he wants to talk to *you* about finding a new broker.

I groaned.

"*I* know. He's not slick. I know his M.O. But business is business, and it is about hooking a sista up. So what do you want me to do?"

I was shuffling into the kitchen, blinking like a mole. "Well, after everything you've told me, I couldn't get it twisted if I wanted to. I'm obviously not a model, and I'm not up for no 'manly man' bullshit. But you're right—business *is* business. Give him my office number, and I'll refer him."

"Good for you. You're grown."

Monday morning before I could have my second cup of coffee and get through the weekend's e-mails, Kurt called. Within half a minute I could tell he didn't want advice on picking a new broker. I played with him for a few minutes but time is money and it was Monday morning.

"So, Kurt, I hope that's helpful. As I said, give Steve in our private client group a call and I'll shoot him an e-mail to let him know you'll be calling."

"Oh, you don't have to do that. I just wanted to do a little baseline research before I jumped in, so I'll hold onto the info until I'm ready to pull the trigger. But thanks—I really appreciate your taking time out to talk with me. And since you've been so helpful, can I reciprocate by inviting you to be my guest Friday night at the Spy Club? We're showcasing a new artist and it should be pretty hot."

"Thanks for the invite, but let me get back to you, say, tomorrow afternoon."

I knew his specs, and I couldn't help but think he was being nice to me to suck up to Olga, but what the hell. It would probably be pretty cool and at worst he'd ignore me—or maybe that would be at best. I could entertain myself in a room of strangers, and of course there were bound to be other men there.

Olga begged to differ, if screaming into the phone can be called "disagreement." "You're standing on the tracks and the train's barreling toward you at top speed! Get off the tracks!!!"

"So does that mean you're not going to coordinate my wardrobe for Friday night?"

"God, you get on my nerves sometimes—of course I am! We'll make you stunning."

Friday after work she came over to do her magic. When it was all said and done I'd cleaned up pretty nicely. Olga did my hair and makeup and dressed me in a little black dress with spaghetti straps and strappy sandals. I might not be a model but I felt like one. Right up until we got to the Spy Club. Within minutes Kurt was surrounded by models. What kind of pheromones was this guy wearing? I, on the other hand, was a magnet for every gray-haired man on the prowl for a young brown somebody. I told myself this was good 'cause it meant I'd be home by midnight, but my bravado was gone. Seeing him enveloped by model beauties stirred up all my insecurities. I felt short, fat, and nearly invisible in a room filled with five-foot-eight waif-thin size-2 women. But between the dirty old men hounding me and some positive self talk (*I'm bright, successful, pretty in a natural way, and my mama loves me*) I managed to not shrink out of the place—I even had an okay time. Then suddenly it was about 1 A.M. and Kurt was across the room, waving for me to come over, though he didn't look ready to go.

"Having a good time?"

"Thanks, it's been cool, but I think I'm going to head out. I'll hop in a cab and be home in ten minutes."

"Oh, no way—and have Olga say I have no home training? She already thinks I'm below dirt. I've had enough, too. Let's roll."

And so it was we became friends; and, kind of, lovers; or, in my uncle's categories, something between fuck buddy and activity pal. He tapped into my love of live music—it was work for him but a blast for me—and I let him do his thing. I was content to hear tunes, be in the mix, and have sort of a date. We'd come in together and leave together. He'd said hanging out with me was keeping him out of trouble and helping clean up his bad boy image. I was only the second woman he'd "hung out" with who was not a model. And, because I'd heard my uncle's words but not listened to them, I took that as a compliment: A man who only dug models dug *me*.

Unfortunately, his affinity for models hadn't died; it just went underground. He subtly went to work finding my insecurities and playing on them. Very gently he'd make suggestions about my hair, my nail polish color, my makeup, making sure I always had the newest copies of *Vogue*, *Glamour* and *InStyle*. He'd surprise me with dresses that even with starvation I'd never fit into. He arranged for a visit with a stylist, a perk of his profession that shouldn't be wasted, and sent me for a day makeover at a spa. I deserved to be pampered he said, and he was right.

Of course, while he was pampering me he was refashioning

me. And I let it happen. He made me feel pretty and special. But within three months my look had changed, and my walk and my talk were changing with it. I'd become consumed with losing weight. It seemed the harder I worked out and the less I ate, the more weight I gained. I was never quite conscious that hanging out all the time, eating late dinners, and being on the edge from work were all making me tired, and it was showing up on my face. Cover-up, eye packs, and cucumbers weren't hiding my dark circles or removing the puffiness from underneath my eyes. And so it went on until the Friday night of the Maxwell concert.

We met at the Aubette for cocktails before the show. After exchanging details of the day and a few Ketel One martinis with olives, Kurt leaned over and kissed me on the forehead. He knew I loved that. Taking my hand, he became very serious, looking me dead in the eyes.

"You know, I've been thinking. You've got the wife qualities I've always wanted. I could see myself marrying you if you got a boob job and dropped another twenty pounds."

I was stunned. I was shocked. But most of all, I was—I know, finally!—offended. It took all my womanhood not to throw my drink at him. I'd never been one for public scenes and I wasn't going to start now. I liked Aubette. I would not give Kurt the pleasure of seeing me wounded and act like a fool. I stood up and walked out the door. I headed down Park Avenue towards Union Square. I needed to walk. I felt like I'd been run over by a bus. Every time he introduced me to someone he'd been thinking—cow? Every time he gave me a hug and kiss goodnight he'd been thinking—pancake? Olga had been right. I was on the tracks and the train clearly hit me.

He caught up to me at Twenty-third Street.

"I'm sorry. I'm so sorry. I don't now what came over me."

"Are you just mean? Do you have Tourette's syndrome? Are you now just showing me how much of an asshole you really are? Or is it *all* of the above? Come on, you're used to making simple choices. Pick one."

"I'm really sorry. I don't now what came over me. Let me make it up to you. Let's just go to the concert."

"You've lost your mind. Clearly you want a Barbie and I'm a Skipper. Don't ever call me again. There are no do-overs."

I left him standing on the corner. I hopped in a cab and cried all the way home. No Maxwell love song would mend my heart. Standing in the mirror I felt ugly. Never before in my life had I felt that way. And then I got mad. Mad that he could hurt me. Mad that although I knew his words didn't really matter it still hurt. Mad that I hadn't heeded Olga's warning. Mad that he could fix his mouth to put "wife qualities," "boob job," and "lose twenty pounds" in the same sentence, and say it to *me*. But then I remembered what Mama had once said. She was doing my hair and getting me dressed for my First Communion.

"There will come a time when you're going to have to remember that you're a princess. Someone will say you're not, but you are. Remember that you are a princess—'cause I said so!" And with that she kissed me on the forehead and swatted my behind.

This was the moment she'd spoken about.

He called to apologize every hour on the hour Saturday and Sunday. I turned the ringer and my cell phone off. There was no need to acknowledge or respond to him. He might as well have given me a black eye. It hurt the same and I knew it would just happen again if I let him back in. Then the flowers began showing up at work and at home. I had more flowers than most funerals or corner delis. They were apropos. I know how corny it sounds, but I really felt like his words had killed a part of me. It had become a funeral for my believing that the dating game was about fun and possibly finding a Prince Charming. I'd never had someone be so utterly inhumane to me. I wanted to analyze him and say it was something deep-seated from his childhood. It was a defense mechanism. But no matter how I mulled it over, it just became clearer that he was an abusive man. He played into my desire to be and feel pretty. I'd allowed him to alter my way of being, although superficially, by the way I looked. It was the setup. I had been sucker punched, lulled into thinking he was interested in me for who I was. That my personality, intelligence, spirituality, sense of family and community, and sense of humor mattered to him. I thought the nights we'd hung out gallivanting around town fostered at least a friendship. But no friend would ever be so hurtful and malicious. I was a Skipper and would never be a Barbie. And that's what I got for playing with a Ken doll.

14

Switch Hitting

My Grandma always said . . .
Keep hitting your head against
that brick wall, and you'll
draw blood

Olga called. "What are you doing tonight? No date? Come on and go with me to Jack's. I don't want to go by myself. He's having a dinner party and you know there'll be men, men everywhere. He asked me to invite you. He wants to even out the ratio of men to women."

"Oh, we'd hate for the ratio to be uneven now, wouldn't we? I'll be at your place in an hour." I was hungry and it wouldn't kill me to be social for a few hours. Dinner and light conversation—not in a bar, not in a restaurant—I could be home before the news was over. Jack threw the best dinner parties. His apartment was spacious, Spoonbread catered dinner, the bartender was cute, and the wine was flowing; it might not be a bad night after all. Jack was the general contractor who renovated Olga's apartment. The job had taken nearly a year to finish during which time he and Olga became friends of a sort. They shared a love of fine things, he introduced Olga to her personal trainer and her investment advisor, and convinced her to attend his church. Jack was grounded, fun, and fine. "I'm so glad your social calendar allowed you to come play with us."

"And miss great grub and rubbing elbows with the beautiful people? Not on your life! As always, everything's wonderful. Thanks for inviting me."

"Let me introduce you to some folks." We headed straight for the corner where six brothers were staring at his wall of "artistic" photos. Jack was a photographer in his spare time and preferred to shoot nudes. It was quite a collection. A rather dorky looking guy in a dress shirt without a tie and nasal voice accosted Jack before he could reach the group. "So tell me," he said, pointing to a picture of two beefcake men and a drugged-out looking woman, "how do you get people to pose for you?"

Jack answered with a devilish grin. "I have my ways. If I told you, I'd have to kill you—or make you pose." The group standing around laughed, and the dorky guy went off toward the kitchen. "Don't pay him any mind. That's Cal. He's got no game—or personality, for that matter. Anyway, guys, let me introduce you. This is Dan, Mel, and Evan. Guys, I told you about Olga's friend . . ."

"Hi guys." I tried to sound interested. Dan and Mel gave me a pleasant hello but returned to their conversation. Evan offered me a glass of wine asking, "So how do you know Jack?"

"He was my friend Olga's contractor. She's holding court with a group of men on the other side of the room. How do you know Jack?"

"We go to the same gym, plus we have an ex in common."

"That sounds like a story."

"Nah, not really—there wasn't any overlap. We were both being played." He changed the subject. "So where do you live?"

"Brooklyn."

"Brooklyn's cool, but I guess I'm a city boy. I live in the East Village—Avenue A and Thirteenth Street, down from Tompkins Square Park."

"Isn't it a little hectic around there?"

"Not any more. The park's been redone, and there are lots of great restaurants, bars, and shops. We'll have to hang out so I can show you the neighborhood."

"That sounds like fun." We chatted on and off throughout the night. *Let's see if he asks for my number.* As we stood off to the side laughing and talking, Olga walked up very buzzed and whispered but in full voice, "I'm not trying to bust your groove, but I've got to go home. I think I had a little too much wine."

"Evan, I guess it's about that time."

"Here, take my card. My home and cell numbers are on the back. Let's hang out soon." I handed him mine. He called Sunday and we met Friday after work for dinner at First. Evan was a great dinner companion. We talked about living in the city, working on the Street, and prep school—turned out he'd gone to a rival school. He was a bond attorney at a downtown firm and shared a triplex with Dan, whom I'd met at Jack's dinner party—they'd been roommates ever since freshman year in college. We made a weekly habit of meeting for dinner nearly every Friday for a while, trying out new and old favorite restaurants around town, and usually spoke with each other once a day. It felt like we were dating, but he kept his distance and never once tried to kiss me. We'd just embrace goodnight with a peck on the cheek. I really didn't think much of it. It was nice to have civilized non–sex starved male company.

One Friday night he invited me to his house to watch the Knicks game and order in sushi. It was the first time I'd been to his place. The triplex had spectacular views of the Chrysler Building to the north. Aside from the views, the space was nondescript and had a boys dorm-room feeling. There wasn't much furniture except for a large-screen TV, a sofa and a putting green in the middle of the living room floor. We sat on the sofa watching the game and eating sushi. It was a quiet night, until Dan came home, pissy drunk and in a rage.

"I've indulged you and this little phase of yours long enough!" Dan screamed, pointing at me. "You have the nerve to bring this trollop into our home? You need to pick a team!"

Evan stood and approached Dan very calmly. "Dan, take your drunk ass to bed."

"Don't tell me what to do. We're gonna settle this right now or I'm leaving for good this time. It's either going to be beef or fish but you can't have both anymore. You're humiliating me."

I'd walked into a mess and needed to get out before it got uglier. It was more than I needed after watching the Knicks lose again. As I picked up my bag and sweater heading for the door Dan lashed into me.

"Oh, now you're going to leave. I guess Mr. Straight Boy won't be getting *any* ass tonight—yours *or* mine." I blinked. "Oh yeah he likes ass, all right—*my* ass!" Dan turned his butt towards my face and shook it. Then he screamed: "Tell her! Tell her the truth!"

Evan's face was as blank as if he were watching a conversation between strangers, at a distance. I stepped in front of him.

"Look, Evan, I don't know what's going on but—"

He cut me off. "Dan's just drunk."

"I'm not drunk. I'm just sick of you lying and cheating."

"Dan, just shut up and go to bed." Turning to me he shoved a twenty into my bag. "You should go. Let me get Dan to bed and let's have brunch in the morning."

"You're joking, right?"

"Let's talk about it in the morning." I left to the sounds of Dan throwing up in the bathroom.

I was dazed leaving the apartment. Hailing a cab at 1:00 A.M., the East Village was alive. People strolling along the park, entering restaurants and bars for a late night snack or drink, hip-hop and club music escaped from open bar doors. My world was spinning. In the cab the waterworks started. I cried all the way home. What had I missed? Was he bi? Was Dan telling the truth? Was Dan really his lover? I just felt stupid. But he was a man's man. It never even entered my mind that he might be gay. How could this be? I had put him in camp possibility. Weren't we on the way to having a relationship? I thought he was just slow. Now this. What was I doing wrong?

I turned off the ringer on my phone. I turned off the cell phone and stayed in bed all day. I didn't want to talk with anyone. This was too much. Had I not asked the critical questions? Had I not been listening, observing? At 5:00 P.M. I got out of bed and checked my messages. I was mad now. Kay, Max, Olga and Bea had called but no Evan. I called Kay.

"You sound like shit. What's wrong?" I started crying again. "I'm on my way over." Kay arrived with cookie dough and Cool Ranch Doritos. She gave me a hug at the door saying, "Oh girl, you look bad. What happened now?" I told her the sordid story of Dan and Evan.

She looked as bewildered as I felt. "Just be glad that now you know. I hate to ask, but did you ever sleep with him?"

"No! I just thought he was a nice guy and moved slow."

"Well, I guess all's well that ends without a visit to the doctor."

"You know Kay, when we met he said he and Jack, Olga's contractor, had an ex in common."

"And you didn't make him elaborate? I wish you'd told me before. I could have told you Jack's on the other team—always has been and always will be."

"You're lying!"

"Most people don't wear their sexuality on their sleeves unless they like to tell *all* their business. It's no one's business who sleeps with whom, unless you're sleeping with *them*."

I opened a beer. Was I so naïve and desperate for male company that I could no longer discern straight from gay, not to mention single from committed? He hadn't lied to me. I never thought to ask, and he didn't tell.

"The facts are the facts. He probably does like men and his roommate was most likely his lover. Think about it this way, Dan knew that you guys were hanging out, and they live together—how do you think *he* feels? Now that's some shit. Evan better be glad that Dan's not a woman. It could have gotten rough, because you and I know a woman would have hurt you *and* him if she had walked in and found another woman up in her house."

Kay was right. I'd just have to get over it. I had walked away relatively unscathed. I'd just have to make sure to check to see who was pitching first.

15

Napkins, Q-Tips, and Other Issues of Hygiene

My Grandma always said . . .
Act like you got a family and
some home training, you weren't
raised in a barn

Olga and Kay had been feeling bad that, instead of getting me "back in the game," dating was hardening my heart and defusing some of my love for life and humanity. So when Olga's husband's college roommate Thomas held a mini-reunion for their fraternity at his home in Cobble Hill, Olga thought it would be a great opportunity for me to possibly meet a "nice normal guy." The ratio of men to women would clearly be skewed in my favor. Armed with a positive attitude, smiles, and the determination to just have a pleasant evening, I decided to join them.

Beyond having to listen to the boys reminisce about their school days and current gossip about who'd recently married, divorced, been promoted or fired, or started their own company, the dinner was mildly entertaining. Men can be worse than women in their criticism of each other. By dessert, everyone had had more than their share of wine. Thomas pulled out a mix tape with the Jungle Brothers, A Tribe Called Quest, De La Sol, Kid'n Play and Public Enemy, and old dances began, with Claude and Thomas leading the crowd of fifteen or so. First it was the Smurf, then the Prep, and then the Running Man. For a moment it almost felt like a college Friday night, except there were more men than women in the room. I cut up pretty furiously with Thomas, Olga, and Claude. At the end of the night we left laughing, remembering the best of college and Thomas even asked for my number. "We should keep in touch." It had been a fun Friday night.

Yes, I had hope—I really did. Dinner parties of friends whose romantic taste and social skills you trust are great opportunities for meeting people. Unfortunately, sometimes what seems like "a catch" can easily turn out to be an engine not running on all cylinders.

Southern, Stanford undergraduate, three years in Asia, Wharton MBA, owner of a small internet company. Resumes and statistics mean nothing. Although the dinner party had been well executed, it became painfully clear that at twenty-nine years old Thomas had never socially developed beyond age fifteen.

Our first date was a formal dinner for a not-for-profit company where he served on the board. All in all it was a pleasant evening, but there are always clues that folks aren't "normal," clues we ignore at our peril. For example: He kept bending down under the table, and I thought he must have been dropping his napkin again and again. Finally I looked over: He had been wiping his mouth with the end of the tablecloth. When the server walked by I asked for another napkin, and placed it near Thomas when it arrived. Nothing doing: He continued to wipe his mouth with the end of the tablecloth. It just seemed strange but I let it go, at my peril.

The next Friday night we decided to have dinner at Mekka, a great Caribbean/Soulfood place at the bottom end of Avenue A. It was warm when he came to pick me up, but he was sweating *profusely*, the sweat pouring from his forehead like someone had poured water over his head. He mentioned that his Friday after-work basketball game ran late, and he'd just come from the gym. In the car I could tell. The wet dog smell overpowered the air freshener. Did he think B.O. was some sort of an aphrodisiac? This was going to be an early evening. I rolled the window down to get some fresh air, but the odor was so strong I had a headache by the time we crossed the bridge into Manhattan. I was afraid *I* would reek by the time we got out of the car.

As soon as we were seated at Mekka Thomas put his feet up in the empty chair next to us. When the waitress asked him to put his feet down, he caught an attitude. "Doesn't she understand that business is about service? Instead of worrying about where I put my feet, she should be concerned about taking our orders. Doesn't she know that I'm hungry?" The impatience and condescension weren't winning him any points with me. Too bad he didn't take his table manners as seriously as his service ethic. But I decided this was another opportunity to practice my own patience.

I'm no Miss Manners but when the first course arrived and

he assumed the position, hunching over the bowl as if he were afraid the other patrons would take it away, I wanted to disappear. Then the slurping began. It was so loud that the waitress came over.

"Is it too hot? You might want to wait till it cools."

"No, it's *not* too hot," he barked. "As a matter of fact, it's not hot at all. I should probably send it back!" And he probably would have too, except that when the three of us looked down at the bowl we could see it was utterly empty—he must have licked it clean. I wrote it off to his stint in Asia, but in no civilized, culture that I'm familiar with is chewing with one's mouth open, snorting like a pig, and moaning "Oh, great food!" considered appropriate table manners. He attacked his plate like it was his first meal in many months, and finished it in under five minutes. I'd lost my appetite and was ready to go. Food dripped from the sides of his mouth. He used the back of his hand to wipe his mouth. I thought it couldn't get any worse, but then he used the napkin to blow his nose and asked me to check his nose to make sure he got it all. I suggested that he excuse himself and check it out in the bathroom, but he declined. I've never witnessed a colon cleansing, but I can't imagine it being worse than watching him eat.

He ordered coffee to settle his devoured meal, poured nearly all the sugar packets on the table into the cup, and drank it with the spoon, slurping. Midway through this process he began scratching his throat, sticking his finger in his ear and swallowing, and making a hacking sound. He removed his finger from his ear, examined the wax, rolled it into a ball, and wiped it on the tablecloth. I'm not making this up. I *wish* I were making this up.

"We should do this again. There's a lot of restaurants I've

been meaning to check out." The thought of having to spend another evening watching him eat made me cringe. I smiled sheepishly and lied through my teeth. "I'm starting a strict diet tomorrow, and I won't be able to eat out for several months. But thanks!" *And if I ever need another barnyard experience, I'll visit a farm.*

16

Social Stepper

My Grandma always said . . .
It's not always what you know,
sometimes it's who you know

Kay called pissed off. "I've had enough of these capped brothers!"

"Girl, what are you talking about? I thought you had a date tonight."

"The man was capped—no bonus payout, no stock options, limited earning potential, no possibility of a golden parachute—capped."

"Oh, not this 'capped' business again! I just don't get who you think would want to support someone? Would you want to date you? Are *you* in any way, shape, or form the person that *you* want to be with? Are you doing and being *any* of the things you'd want your significant other to do or be? I mean, how are you clocking someone's ride when you're still taking the bus? How are you sweating someone's crib when you're still renting and don't have $1000 in the bank?"

"Oh, well, excuse me, I guess I forgot who I called. You're *always* meeting some banker or lawyer or doctor. I just want someone who's my equal."

"Kay, what does that even *mean,* your 'equal'? Do you honestly believe that men are your equal?"

"No. Of course not."

"Then what are you really talking about?"

"Well, I've been trying to give the average man a chance. You know, the average hardworking guy—police officer, fire-fighter, construction worker—the everyday type of person, but they're full of shit too. I've been periodically going out with Greg. We've been going to the movies, bowling, and the arcade, light low-key fun. He seemed pretty cool, and it was refreshing—no flossing, no shoptalk, no fabulousness. So last night we're supposed to go to the movies again at 7:30. I bust my behind to get home and pull it together but by eight o'clock, no call, no show, no nothing. I called him at home and on his cell. No answer. So by eleven I was good and mad and just got ready for bed. At 12:30 he calls to say he got 'caught up,' and wanted to know if he could come over, like I was some booty call! When I told him no, he got all nasty—saying I was stuck up, boring, and frigid."

"Oh, no he didn't!" I could tell she was more pissed off than hurt, so I was happy to encourage her little rant.

"Oh, yes he did! I told him to go find some ho if that's what he wanted, but he still wasn't coming to my house!"

"You go!"

"I am not interested in sleeping with someone just because

we go out a few times and had some fun. Whatever happened to courting? Whatever happened to people taking time to get to know each other before jumping into bed? We went out about ten times, and I bet he doesn't even know my favorite color. I went to sleep and decided to call this morning before I went to work to see what his problem was last night."

"You *what?*"

"Just be quiet. Anyway, some babe answered the phone and he had the nerve to say to me, 'Well you didn't want me to come over last night!'—like it was my fault! I knew we weren't seeing each other exclusively, but damn—give me some respect! See? That's what I get for doing charity work."

"Now look, Kay, if you thought it was charity work in the first place, that's already a problem. But if you're interested in more than jumping into bed, that makes sense. We all need to date more intentionally if we're serious about not being single forever. But what happened to Blake? I thought things were moving along."

"Him? He's tired. All he wants to do is be in the mix. We've been there, done that. Every party or event where he thinks everyone is going to be, he's there. He only wanted me to go with him because he thinks other people think it's cool that we hang out. Like last week we went to dinner with a bunch of people, half of whom I don't even think he knows, and then went to some banker's party uptown. He was so busy being Mr. Social Superfly that when I said I was leaving and I'd had enough of pretending I was having a good time, he didn't even hear me. He called me at 3:00 A.M. all pissed off that I'd left. People asked him if we were having a fight. He didn't have a response because he didn't *notice* that I was gone! He's more concerned about what other people think than he is about what I think, but if he ever needed $20, he surely couldn't call on any of those people whose opinions he's so concerned about. I swear—give a brother a few degrees and a decent job, they swear they're doing something."

"Wait up a sec. I thought that's what you *wanted*—some banker or lawyer who was social and paid, who wanted to hang out with you."

"I do want that but it just seems like they are all superficial and full of themselves."

"Kay, come on. You and I both know that there's no love connection made on the dance floor in the club or standing in line at a token booth."

"So what am I supposed to do?"

"Well, if I knew, don't you think I'd be doing it too?"

"Hm! Speaking of dates, why are *you* home tonight?"

"I'm going running with Jason in the morning."

"Oh *really?*"

"Don't get excited. We're just friends. Anyway, when I meet Prince Charming I'll be sure to introduce you to his brothers, cousins, or friends. Until then, you want to go to the movies?"

17

Somebody Else's Shoes

My Grandma always said . . .
Shoes too small for your feet
will give you corns.

We first met a few years ago, at a
mutual friend's Super Bowl party. Occasionally
we'd run into each other at parties and in
Prospect Park. We'd have very upbeat, general-
acquaintance-type conversations about work
and recent sightings of mutual friends, and our
encounters would end with "Great to see you!
Hope to run into you again soon!" I was always
happy to run into him, certainly to look at him:
At six foot one, creamy, dark chocolate skin,
long and lean, with broad yet defined features,
Jason is undeniably handsome.

When he walked into Kay's annual New Year's Day fish fry, I couldn't remember the last time I'd seen him. We exchanged pleasantries as always, but this time he was unusually chatty. I chalked it up to too many beers. As the evening wore on he managed to keep finding a seat near me, refreshing my drink, and bringing me snacks as we watched the game. At first I didn't read anything into it, since he'd been seeing Elena for nearly two years. But as I was leaving, he handed me his card and said, "Let's get together for coffee or drinks." I took his card, smiled and murmured, "Sure, that'd be great," thinking, *Yeah, right. I'm sure Elena would just love that.* I stuck the card in the bottom of my bag.

After Kay's dinner it seemed like I was running into him at least twice a week—in the bank, at the farmers' market, running in the park, on the subway platform—and each time he suggested we get together, as if he'd never mentioned it before. Three weeks later he caught me off guard one Saturday morning as I was running errands, so I finally agreed to have a quick coffee with him.

On this particular Saturday morning a headache had woken me early from a night of fitful sleep. The night before I'd gone out with a nice guy for the third time. Just as we were about to kiss goodnight for the first time, he stopped and launched into a long speech about how guilty he felt, and how he'd really liked me and would love to spend more time with me, but (big but) he was seeing someone else who lived in another city . . . He stood on my stoop going on about the situation for almost twenty minutes, trying to rationalize our previous "dates."

Believe it or not, I didn't see this one coming. Ouch! But his honorable confession was all it took. We were over before we began.

Damn. I felt a little sad, and also a little pissed that he'd misled me. But I wasn't interested in some kind of "arrangement"—it's always a slippery slope when you spend serious time with someone you know is dating someone else. Eventually something will happen—the other person will find out and people will get hurt. Whatever might have been wasn't worth the drama.

So Saturday morning found me in front of the flower stall, debating between sunflowers or tiger lilies to cheer myself up when Jason walked up beside me.

"Go for the tiger lilies. They're you." His smile and his easy manner knocked me off track from my brooding—and choosing my flowers. "Hey, let me treat you to a coffee. Don't tell me you can't spare twenty minutes out of your day." What a cute grin. He was completely disarming.

The conversation started like all our previous ones until he asked point blank, "Hey, how come you never called me after Kay's party?"

The question took me by surprise, but I had a simple answer. I folded my arms across my chest. "Well. Let's see. Last I heard, you were seeing Elena. And I make it a point not to go out with guys who are involved." After the previous night, it felt good to stand on terra firma.

He folded his arms too and looked serious. "Elena and I have started seeing other people. Things haven't been working out between us for a while."

I couldn't hide my suspicion. "That's sad, but why don't you just break up?"

He shrugged. "Letting go is a process. Anyway, you know as well as I do that the dating game is drama. We're cool and we still hang out, and we both know this wasn't leading to marriage. I think we're trying to figure out how to help each other be happy."

The headache that woke me came back, but this time it brought along a friend—my queasy stomach. I thought about Grandma saying, "How you find them is how you lose them."

I guess I was not wearing my discomfort on my sleeve, because he kept right on going. "We should get together. Maybe go running? How about a run around Grand Army Plaza next Saturday?"

I couldn't tell if he was real smooth, or for real, so I said yes despite my queasy stomach. Hell, I run every other day anyway. Running with him won't be any more dangerous than having a cup of coffee. Absolutely harmless. I'd been burned by the rebound shuffle before, and I wasn't about to rush into anything with anyone who was just ending a relationship.

A week later we go for a run, and it's harmless, so we run again the week after that. After a couple of weeks he suggests a midweek run, and our harmless runs go from once a week to twice a week without my really noticing. The next thing I know, we're spending Saturdays together—all day, every week. On the surface we're strictly platonic. But somehow Saturday is becoming "sacred time" and I find myself looking forward to it. We run, recap and update each other on the week's events, eat brunch, run errands together, and in the afternoon and evenings we walk around arm in arm and always hug good-bye.

I slowly stopped watching him for signs of rebound. After all, we weren't lovers, so what difference did it make? Instead I felt like we were becoming good friends, and anyway I knew that, no matter what he said, it would take him a few months to get over Elena. Once in a while he'd tell me about one of their many arguments and his fear of committing. Then we'd talk about my own inability to find anyone I'd want to commit to, and my endless succession of sometimes funny, sometimes bizarre, dates.

Friday night we decided to skip the run and just meet for dinner. When I got to his apartment, he was cooking, but he wasn't as talkative as usual. When I asked what was eating him, he said he was just tired, so I let it alone. But as we ate he would stare out the window, then at me, then out the window again. I was trying to hold up my end of the dinner conversation, but he kept dropping his. About midway through dinner the queasy feeling from our first coffee came back. We cleared the table and I headed for the bathroom.

I turned on the bathroom light, and there they were—red leather mules. I could see at a glance that they were slightly worn, so no chance they were a surprise gift for me. Then, in one of the strangest moments of my life, without thinking about it I slipped my feet into them, like I was Dorothy in a warped version of *The Wizard of Oz*. Of course they didn't fit—too long and too narrow for my little feet.

Queasy turned to nauseous.

Then it hit me. Knowing he was on the rebound, I was so busy not rushing things that I didn't realize how hard I was falling for him. A wave of pure jealousy almost knocked me over. He was dating someone already and it wasn't me! I took a deep breath and walked into the kitchen, forcing a smile. "So when did you start wearing red leather mules?"

His look said everything, but he rambled on a mile a minute anyway. "Look, I know when we started hanging out this was a 'let's see what happens' kind of thing. I'm very attracted to you, and I really like you but I've still got some stuff to work out with Elena, stuff I thought was done, and I don't want to drag you through it. I know you've dated and hung out with a lot of guys who haven't always been up-front with you, and I want to be different 'cause I really respect you and I don't want you to lose your respect for me. But next weekend we're, uh, Elena and I, we're going to Paris for the weekend. She stayed over last night. We've been talking, trying to work things out. . . . I hope you don't think I've taken advantage of you, 'cause I've loved the time we spent together and I want to be completely honest with you . . . and I feel bad because you're really fun, and really cool, and . . ."

He was still *seeing* Elena? Romantically? It took a few seconds for his words to sink in, and when they did my next impulse was pure ghetto. Throw the coffee at him—the face, go for the face! I had to stop and breathe. I felt like the sucker who'd just discovered her first-class cruise was on the Titanic.

When I could finally speak I kept it simple. "Jason. I appreciate your honesty. I value your friendship. If you ever need anything, please call me. And let me know how you're doing, once in a while." My monotone would have made Data sound like a Master Thespian.

He winced. "You make it sound like this is it."

"Well . . . it is. I can't pretend we're not attracted to each other. But you've got stuff to figure out. I thought you and Elena were 'letting go,' and now you're going to Paris. That's not how I'd let someone go."

To this day I've never figured out why people in relationships—seeing someone regularly, living with someone, or flat-out married—try to date other people. If someone out there claims you and it works for you to claim that someone, you are in a *committed* relationship. There's no room for someone else.

We hugged good-bye. Walking out of his building and down Seventh Avenue I felt like crying. In several months of dating I hadn't come closer to finding someone I love who loves me. I had gotten over Luke, but I hadn't stepped fully out of the loop of romantic betrayal. Then it hit me clearer than it ever had before. Why did I have to go and try on someone else's shoes? I want my own shoes. I want new shoes I can take out of the box and walk a few miles in. And even if they give me blisters along the way, they're my shoes and they fit my feet. And when I take them off, they'll be in a safe place where no one else will try them on.

"God watches out for

babies and fools"

18

CFA (Chartered Fantasy Affliction)

My Grandma always said . . .
It ain't enough to have some book sense;
you better have some common sense.

I'd been attempting to take back my Friday nights and my life, but the dating game really wasn't doing it for me. I was tired of bars and clubs and parties. I was tired of hoping that each new man I met might be that someone who would like me for me. I was tired of putting myself on the line, opening myself up only to have some nitwit man disregard my feelings, and my body for that matter. I was tired of the game. I no longer had the energy or the desire to continue the dating/mating dance. My feet were being too hurt too often. So I decided that it was time for me to truly focus on myself. I decided to take the level one Chartered Financial Analyst (CFA) examination.

Taking the level one CFA exam was more than a notion—sixty percent of the people who take the exam fail the first time. It would require that I study for at least six months and keep to a rigorous study and review course regimen to learn the required material. But after the last few rounds of the dating game, the solitude of studying was a welcome change. But life has a funny way of always reminding you of your heart's true desires, and studying for the CFA exam was one of those funny ways.

"Excuse me, could you show me how to calculate present value on the HP 2C? I think I missed a function when the instructor was going through it."

I guess my wrinkled forehead, pursed lips, and rolling eyes, made him ask again.

"It would only—"

I cut him off, flat, dry, and annoyed. "Sure. Two seconds."

The level one CFA exam day was rapidly approaching. I was still trying to *learn* the material covered on the exam, forget memorizing it. So how is it that *I* end up playing teacher, crossing guard, or caretaker? It amazes me that in a so-called "man's world" men are always asking women for things they could do or figure out for themselves.

"Let me show you." Leaning over, I was glad I'd showered and sprayed on a little Clinique Happy before class that morning. "What's the interest rate? Five percent. See the top of the register? Those are the keys you'll use to do the calculation. What's the payment? What's the time period? Press the PV key. Got it? Now you do it."

"Okay, let's see—you did this, this, this, this . . . I got it! Thanks. I might pass after all."

"*Only* if you pay attention and study!"

He lowered his head like a kicked puppy for a second, then flashed a grin. "Would you like to join me for dinner? I'd love to review this evening's class with you. There's a great place in Battery Park that makes excellent turkey burgers. You game?"

Collecting my notebook, highlighters, pens, and calculator, I thought to myself, *treat them mean and they always seem to like it.* Well, I could either go home and spend another Friday night half studying, half replaying the what's-wrong-in-my-life tape in my head, or have dinner with this random man from my review class. "Are you talking about the American Park Café, or the burger guy by the 4 main entrance?"

He laughed. "What do you know about the burger guy? You don't look like the type to eat from street vendor carts."

"And what's that supposed to mean?"

"Ah, let's just say you look like the linen napkin type."

"And what's the 'linen napkin type'? You want to try that again?"

"You're always so put together."

I gave him a look.

"What? You think I just randomly invite women to dinner? I've noticed you in class. Everyone else either rushes in Fridays after work, looking like they have to find quarters for the meter before the car gets booted, or they straggle in like they'd rather be getting a root canal or doing laundry than sitting in class on a Friday night. You're always crisp, bright-eyed, focused, and intense. For God's sake, you ask questions at 8:00

P.M. when everyone is counting down the seconds until class is over. You cook with gas!"

"Maybe I do, maybe I don't. Anyway, which is it—the American Park Café or the burger guy?

"I guess you'll have to come along and see."

I love even the most basic intrigue, and if he thought I was the linen napkin type and "cooked with gas" and wanted to have dinner, well, it was his choice. We're all adults, right?

It was a brisk evening and the wintry gale off the Hudson betrayed any hopes for warm. Walking from the World Financial Center promenade, through JFK Park en route to the American Park Café, I sensed a mini-adventure budding.

"What a lovely evening! The Statue of Liberty is just simply majestic. I can only imagine how jubilant my grandparents must have been when they arrived from Ireland to Ellis Island and saw her for the first time." We stopped to take in Lady Liberty.

I broke the silence. "Ever been to the top? I wonder if it's open at night. I've lived in New York for more than ten years and I haven't been to the top since a field trip in seventh grade. Let's go!" Whoa, wait—was that *me* talking?

"You know, I've *never* been to the top." He smiled and let out a giggle. "I could tell that there was something way-cool about you."

I guess I was supposed to be flattered that he found me "way-cool." I rolled my eyes and smirked. So off we went to find the ferry to the Statue like two twelve-year-olds on a search-and-destroy mission to knock down a beehive.

"By the way, what's your name?"

"Joey—uh, Joseph."

"As in the technicolor dreamcoat."

He broke out into an off-key rendition of the theme song from the musical.

Silencing him, I started applauding, "Thanks for sharing, but don't give up your day job."

"Tough crowd Ms . . . That's Ms. right?"

I winked. "Ah, on a Friday night, you very well could be with, say, Mrs. Jones."

"Mrs. Jones, Mrs. Jones, Mrs. Jones . . . we've got a thang . . . going on . . ."

"What do you know about Mrs. Jones?"

"Oh, come on. You think white boys from Michigan don't know anything about good music? They played that song at my high school prom. I guess I'm dating myself."

"Indeed you are. So that makes you about . . ."

With the indignation of a seven-year-old mistaken for five, he said, "To be exact, I'm thirty-nine."

"And how many days? Are you sure? I'd never have known. You're aging well." I'd have given him maybe thirty, no more than thirty-three. The square chin, chiseled profile, blue sapphire eyes, loose brown curls, and smile of cat that swallowed the canary was still a baby face. A JFK junior look-alike. He'd looked pretty hip in charcoal cords and sweater, sporting leather boots, and a non-biker leather jacket.

"Thanks. It's vitamin E, Viagra, and the young wife."

I choked and snorted. "Really!"

He blushed. "Just kidding."

We were marching towards the ferry. "You still haven't told me your name, Ms . . ." I told him my name, and he immediately began singing the Beatles' song.

"You're such a songbird."

Taking and kissing my hand, "What can I say? I'm pleased to make your acquaintance."

"Well, thank you."

Lady Liberty was closed for renovations, so there wouldn't be any climbing to the top—so much for spontaneity. The view from the American Park Café was just as good. He pulled out my chair and placed the napkin in my lap, saying, "a chair and linen napkin for you." After ordering turkey burgers with fried onions and fries, we talked and laughed for about three hours. A great conversationalist, Joey told stories about catching a ten-pound bass, sharing a cab with Dizzy Gillespie, and playing college football in the Orange Bowl. We swapped nun stories from Catholic grade school, locations of clean bathrooms in the city, and recipes for bistro dishes.

Damn, it had been a long time since someone's conversation really entertained and delighted me. He was easy to talk with and easy on the eyes. He listened as though his life depended on every word I spoke. He asked me thoughtful, but not too intrusive and not too superficial, questions about my life. Sitting across the table from him I felt interesting, attractive, and even sexy. It had been a while since I'd actually felt *anything*, let alone attractive or sexy. I wanted to pinch myself. With the view of Lady Liberty in the foreground, sitting across from this man, I found myself fantasizing about what it would be like having him in my life.

"Joey, it's time for me to go."

"What are you going to do now—go home, roller-set your hair, and read the chapters for next Friday's class?"

"Since you mention it, that sounds like a great idea."

"Can I come? I'm pretty good at putting in the hairpins."

"Thanks, but no thank you. Do I know you?"

"Well, we just spent the evening together. But it could turn into a lifetime." He paused long enough for the words to resonate, then, "Just kidding!" He smiled like an altar boy who sipped too much wine at communion.

"It's time for the check."

"It's my pleasure. Consider it a thank you for the PV calculation."

For the first time in a long time I felt special. "Joey, thank you. I enjoyed dinner."

"Good. Does that mean we can do this again?"

"Perhaps."

"What kind of answer is that?"

"An answer."

"Since you're not going to give me a real answer, can I call you a car, drop you off, take you home?"

"Would you like to rephrase that?"

"Well, it wouldn't be a bad idea to take you home, but—" I don't know what my face said to that, but it must have read my mind because he backed up fast. "I'm sorry. That was over the line. What I meant was, may I offer you a ride to your next destination?"

"No, no thanks. I'll be home in ten minutes."

"How about grabbing supper and studying together next Friday night, after class?"

"Hmmm . . . all right. Now, see? That's what 'perhaps' means."

"Got it. Here are my numbers. Give me your e-mail and we'll confirm on Wednesday."

Had he read *The Rules?* Probably. But I could stand a mini-adventure and wouldn't mind the company, especially if we were studying. We had the same goal in mind—passing the exam. Besides, I had more fun than I'd had in weeks and it was nice to be secretly excited. But if he didn't e-mail me on

Wednesday I'd work it out. I had work to do. JFK Jr. look-alike or not, the exam was looming. Wednesday morning when I logged on there was an e-mail from Joey, time-stamped 12:01 A.M.

"Hope your week is going well. Looking forward to dinner and studying on Friday. I've already finished chapters ten through fifteen. Shall we go to the Met Café? It stays open late on Fridays. It's usually quiet, and anyway you don't know me well enough to come to my place."

I wrote back: "Sounds like a plan."

He thought I was smart and wanted to study. Right?

Friday morning I had a wardrobe moment. Naturally, I called Kay.

"Help! I need fashion assistance! I've got to go to work and then meet Joey to study after class."

"You sound like you're in high school. When did you make this date?"

"It's not a date. We're studying. He's in my review class. We set it up on Wednesday, Miss Rules."

"Thou protestest too much, and providest too much information. Have you bought anything new lately?"

"You know the answer's No. I'm closing on my apartment any day now!"

"Fine. You need to look cute and ladylike—long black skirt, cream ribbed turtleneck, black boots, leather blazer. And leave the luggage at home—no briefcase, and not that huge bucket bag that looks like you're running away from home. Bring the Kate Spade shoulder bag to hold your notebook. He'll have his books. Wear your hair down—no bun. And put on some eye makeup besides that black eyeliner!"

"But I *like* my Soho Bag. We've been all over the world together. And it's cold—I'll freeze my ass off with just a leather blazer on."

"Who are you trying to be, Sally Study-Girl? You're killing me. How many Pashmina shawls do you own? Just tie your black sweater around your neck in the office. It'll keep your professional image intact."

"All right, thanks, you're the best!" Of course by now I was late and I hadn't even turned the curling iron on yet. Was I tripping on something? This is *JUST* studying.

I got dressed, curled my hair, and put my makeup on in a record twenty-five minutes. I was on time. The day whizzed by from conference call to conference call, more assignments, more meetings, and more work. I looked up—it was suddenly 5:30. Shit! Now I was going to be late for class. A cab was outside the office as I walked out.

I got there just as the instructor began and had to sit in the front row. Throughout class I tried my subtle best to turn around and scan the room, but no Joey. Were we still on? As 8:30 approached I realized I'd gotten my hopes up again and the disappointment and the negative self-talk began to set in: *No wonder I'm single—I believe every man I meet could be the one. If he treats me the way I'm supposed to be treated, with respect and kindness, I get it all twisted, thinking he's actually interested in dating me. I'm tripping. What would someone like him want with me? I'm just a little brown girl who happened to have a few lucky breaks and be smart enough to capitalize on them. Besides, even brothers haven't been digging me. Why would some nearly forty-year-old white man be interested in me for who I am? I'm just tripping . . .*

The negative diatribe continued all the way down in the elevator from the fortieth floor. By the time I reached the Liberty Street exit I had worked myself into a funk so blue it could pass for black. I needed to walk to clear my head so I could refocus and study. As I headed up Broadway, Joey greeted me with a forehead kiss followed by a gentle and unassuming kiss squarely on my lips.

I blushed.

"Breathe, butterfly."

How was I supposed to breathe after seductive kisses like those and getting called butterfly? "What happened to you? I didn't see you in class."

"You looked for me? I'm touched."

"Silly! Are we still studying this evening?"

"Of course we are. That's why I'm here. I figured you'd walk this way. I took my chances."

"I see. Do you still want to go to the Met Café?"

"Well, I was thinking maybe we could walk up to Bubby's."

"That'll work." The negative conversation in my head subsided as we walked through TriBeCa. At Bubby's—a homey, friendly place that feels like it's been there since before the neighborhood was cool—we ordered snacks and mochas and got down to work. He was all business. I was pleased that this was work and not play; at least, I think I was pleased. After three hours of grilling each other, reviewing formulas and accounting rules, he leaned back in the chair, teetering on two legs. "It's all fun and games until you break your neck."

Then he swiveled the chair as if he was falling, only to catch himself at the last possible second. "Help, I've fallen," he said, grinning, "and I can't get up." Then he stared me in the eye, not smiling at all. "That is, I've fallen for you. Will you save me?"

I heard a nervous titter that I wished hadn't come from me. "*Mahogany*, right?"

"I'm serious. Do you ever let your guard down? Does anyone ever get inside that wall? Do you *know* how to be vulnerable?" Uh-oh—a productive night of studying was about to get dicey.

"What are you taking about? You think I have a wall up? I beg to differ Mr. Joey. My spider-sense tells me I'm being fed a line."

"I wish you could see you in the world. You'd see what I see. I remember being where you are. One day you'll understand."

What *was* this shit? I was so not digging his condescending tone. I stood up to head for the ladies' room and regroup, and he stood with me as if he was about to reach to embrace me. "I'll be waiting with bated breath." Oh, why? He could have just not liked me. He could have liked me in a normal I-like-you sort of way. Why did it have to be weird?

In the bathroom I took a few deep breaths, and reapplied my lipstick. It was time to go home. When I got back from the bathroom he was waiting, with all our notes and books packed up.

"Let's blow this joint. I have a surprise for you."

"I have to get home."

"Come on, it's Friday night—live a little. You like Japanese food? You'll love this place. I've had reservations for over a month to get in here."

He hailed a cab and off we went to Sugiyama. The place only seats twenty. By the end of the seventh course of some of the most exotic creations I've ever consumed and the fifth bottle of cold sake, the drunken man's tongue spoke the truth of the sober man's mind. He was the "black sheep" of the family. Joey was an arbitrager. He'd gone to business school to escape the family business, and afterward spent seven years as an M&A banker, until he structured the sale of the family business and retired at thirty-five. For the past four years he'd been purchasing rental properties and trading his own account to keep his skills sharp, but he no longer worked for monetary gain: It was for something to do. The CFA exam was just another challenge, another deal to close to keep his skills sharp.

While he was on a truth-telling roll, he told me he'd always preferred women of color, though where they were from didn't matter—Dominican Republic, Jamaica, Puerto Rico. His first wife had been Brazilian. They'd married right out of business school but the pressure of two career-driven people with families that hated each other was too much for them, and it ended after two years.

Listening to him, it seemed to me that most of the choices in his life were about being different for difference's sake, and pissing off his family. He liked the attention of being seen *as* different or *with* different—it was his power game. He didn't want to be just another snot-nosed rich playboy. He wanted to be truly worldly, and desired by all types of women.

"The women of color I've dated are stand-up, quick-witted, sassy, and sexy, and not in some contrived *Cosmopolitan*/Victoria's Secret way. The women are authentic, robust, and sensual. They're living full lives, not waiting for Prince Charming to ride in and swoop them up onto some white horse. They're not looking to marry me after the third date. And I have to admit, I've always been a better boyfriend than husband. I don't do the day-to-day very well."

I looked into myself for a truly appropriate response, and came up with, "Wow. That's a lot." It was a Friday night after a long week, and after downing more food and alcohol in one sitting than I'd consumed in the previous week, I was in no shape to come up with anything better; I blame it on the dreaded post-ethnic-dining syndrome. Luckily it was already time to go.

Leaving the restaurant, on Fifth Avenue, he picked me up and spun me until I was dizzy and giggling. Holding me in his arms, he kissed me. It was like I'd never been kissed before. I didn't want to stop kissing him. I traced his lips with my fingertips. I smiled the entire way home and fell asleep remembering the warmth of his embrace and our kiss.

We agreed to meet the next afternoon to study at the Grand Army Plaza library. He snuck a mocha and a power bar into the library to get me through our study session. Sitting next to me, every twenty minutes he'd pass me a note.

Note 1: "I'm sorry you're green and hung over today. I promise no more sake on a study night. Scout's Honor."

Note 2: "You wear green well." He drew a smiley face.

Note 3: "I had a great time last night."

Note 4: "Want hangover food after studying? Circle yes or no."

Was I in third grade again? It felt like it. I had decided to study for this exam to work on me. But it made sense to me—finance was a male-dominated field, so there was bound to be at least one datable man in the class; I was *bound* to meet a new and different breed of datable men. For once I was just going to see what would happen.

I was enthralled, and from what I could tell, I wasn't the only one. We spent every Friday night, Saturday, and Sunday before the exam together studying, finding places in the city where we could study and talk. We ate and drank—a *lot*. I think I gained ten pounds, and I didn't even mind—I was loving every minute we spent together. I thought about him constantly. The strangest things would make me want to talk with him. Eating beets reminded me of the stories he told about helping in his grandfather's garden as a little boy.

I'd never been so excited to see someone every time we scheduled to meet. I'd hear his voice on my voice mails and long to see him. His smile, the crisp blue of his eyes that seemed to transform to blue-green in dim light. The smell of his skin—fresh and clean, but spicy like cumin. Whenever he spoke I'd imagine outlining his lips with my fingertip, tracing the lines of his mouth, catching his words in my hand. We studied, flirted, and made out in public places. For all my hatred of PDA, with him I didn't care what people thought. People tended to do a double-take when they saw us together anyway—the little brown woman with the JFK look-alike. Cab drivers, waitresses, store clerks, bartenders, and chatty strangers often commented that we seemed ridiculously happy and comfortable together, even madly in love. It only fueled my fantasy about what it would be like having him in my life.

But as exam day approached, we studied more and frolicked less. The night before the exam we had an early dinner at Candela. Both of us were focused and tense. We said very little at dinner and just enjoyed watching the other. Saturday morning we met for breakfast before beginning the daylong exam. Once again we talked very little, but we agreed to meet in front of the Javits Center after the exam. We planned to drive out to Sag Harbor for lobsters. It was game day, and afterwards would be time to return to our "normal lives"—

whatever that meant. We had spent virtually the last three months together. Now what?

At 6:00 P.M. the exam was over, and I was mentally and physically drained. I waited for Joey in front of the center. And waited. At 6:30 there was still no sign of him. I called his cell phone. No answer. I checked mine. No message. I called my sister to kill time.

"Bea? I'm done!"

"Congrats, sweetie. How do you think you did?"

"Let's just pray I passed."

"Are you going out to celebrate?"

"I'm waiting for my, guess you could call him my study buddy, but it's been nearly thirty minutes and I haven't heard from or seen him."

"Maybe he's in the bathroom. You said it was grueling. Are you sure you're in the right place?"

Bea and I chatted until 7:00 P.M., but still no Joey. Maybe I had the plan all wrong. I just headed home. He'd call, right? But by 1:00 A.M. it finally sank in. He wasn't going to call. I was so exhausted, I was nauseous. My head ached. My tears burned in my eyes. I felt like a complete fool, a silly, stupid little ignorant girl. What was I tripping on? JFK look-a-likes don't go for little brown round girls like me, except as something to do or for a proverbial "walk on the wild side." Didn't I learn this lesson in college?

Joey had hit a nerve I didn't know I had. I guess my quick wit and sassiness were only half the fun. Once I met his criterion of forbidden fruit, the other half was the challenge of enticing me to let down my guard. I had never called him. Whenever I was wondering if I should, he'd always call or e-mail me. We'd always met out somewhere. He did not come to my house and I didn't go to his. This was too much. At 4:00 A.M. I just went to bed and cried myself to sleep.

Sunday came and went with no word from Joey. I'd call and only reach his voice mail. I sent him an e-mail but it bounced back. A week passed. Three weeks passed. Nothing. He'd just vanished. I just didn't get it. He just disconnected. He left a hole in my life. Not only was I not consumed with studying for the exam, I no longer had outings with him to look forward to. Had I imagined our relationship? Had all the time we'd spent together meant nothing? Was it all so ephemeral?

Three months later a certified letter arrived in my office. It enclosed a copy of his exam results, a gift certificate for a spa day at Carapan, and a note:

> You *are* the linen napkin type.
> I'm the back of the hand.
> Hanging out with you while studying was grand.
> Now I'm on to Level 2.
> Stay cool and fun.
> Someday your prince will come.
> Thanks again. Best always.
>
> *Joey.*

What had I expected? When I thought about it, we had been only study buddies. I'd created a relationship in my head. The exam was over and that was that. I'd been playing fantasy relationship, like fantasy football. But the season was over and we weren't going to the playoffs.

19

A Pair and a Spare

My Grandma always said . . .
A mouse with only one hole to run
into is a poor mouse.

I always wanted to believe I was a one-man woman. Players juggle multiple women, but I wasn't interested in being a female player, stringing men along or playing both ends against the middle. I just wanted *my* person: someone who wanted me and no one else, someone who would feel that I was enough for him—sass, hips, small boobs, and all. No checklist, no molding me, no soulmate hocus-pocus: He would understand that I am an asset to his life, his growth, and personal development. And he would just love me for who I am.

But I was starting to think that dating more than one person at a time had a few advantages—besides never being home alone. It could keep me from getting too serious too soon, or obsessing on whether he called when he said he would, or whether we had plans for the weekend. Options gave me not only a sense of freedom to choose, but a sense of empowerment. They let me maintain some perspective and some dignity. I wouldn't become too clingy or possessive. Options helped slow the pace of getting to know a guy.

While I was contemplating my options, Kay called.

"Friday night you're coming to my singles mixer. You need to get out more."

"Last I checked I was doing all right. If you want me to come because you don't want to go alone just say so. But I'm not really in the mood to spend my Friday night having trite conversation with a bunch of overeager men. If that's what I wanted, I'd just go to Aubette on Tuesday night."

Kay had recently signed up for an exclusive dating service that held quarterly mixers, and she was on a mission to get me to sign up. I think she might even get a discount on her monthly fee if she enlisted others. Even so, I couldn't help but admire her willingness to continuously date in the quest to find a mate. The dating service was only the latest tactic in a relentless war.

"This is completely different. All the men there are single, employed, and looking for a serious relationship. That's the beauty of it, less stiffing through the mess. Besides you never know, it's like Lotto—you gotta play to win."

"Well, I'll need a bit of motivation if I'm going to come. How about we turn it into a game?" Kay didn't say anything, so I went on, winging it. "We have to exchange numbers with at least five guys, and go out dates with at least two within the next month." I thought Kay would hate the idea and that would be the end of that. But no—she practically squealed with delight.

"That's a great idea! That's why I love you. And whoever wins treats the other to a spa day at Carapan, and if we both win—or we both lose—then we'll just treat each other. Deal?"

"Kay, I was joking."

"No, we're on. Be ready by eight." She hung up before I could say anything else. Serves me right, too.

We arrived at the W Hotel in midtown. The lobby and bar were packed with singles wearing name tags. I was slightly in awe of the sheer numbers of people—old, young, black, white, Asian, well dressed, jean-and-sneaker clad. At the welcome table, a woman who reminded me of my Brownies den mother handed us name tags and explained the icebreaker game everyone was supposed to be playing. She didn't know that Kay and I had our own game going.

She spoke in a soft but stern voice. "Ladies, here are your words for tonight." She handed me a small pad with tear-off strips with the word *some* written on them and handed Kay a set with the word *self*. "Tonight's game requires you to find gentlemen whose suffixes complement your prefixes." She seemed as pleased with herself as if she'd invented the game.

Kay was not pleased in the least, "What kind of prefix is this? Can I pick another?

Our den mother for the night just smiled. "Only one card per guest. Have a good time, ladies!"

Kay was pouting. I offered to switch words with her. She refused.

"Come on, Kay, it's only just a game."

"I know," she huffed, "but what will the word *self* say to a potential suitor?"

"Kay, I have full faith in your ability to work it out." And before I could say anything else, two striking older men (nearly sixty) approached us.

"I'm *bone* and he's *way*." The less attractive of the two introduced them. He looked like a retired used car salesman, toupee and all.

I gestured toward Kay. "And Ms. *self* over here thought she had an odd word. By the way, I'm *some*."

The used car salesman elbowed his friend. "I bet she is!"

Kay was not amused. "Well, *bone* and *way* say it all. I guess we're just no match for you. Bye-bye!" She pulled me away from them.

"Oh, Kay! Easy, playa—they're just little old men!"

"Old dirty bastards, more like," Kay mumbled.

"Boy, where's your sense of humor tonight? This is a singles event and you're taking it much too seriously. This was your idea, remember? I'm heading to the bathroom. I'll be back."

When I returned, Kay was back in form, holding court with three very handsome guys, all of them staring down into the deep V-neck of her sweater. I could tell I was on my way to treating her to Carapan without contest until a very cute man nearly knocked me down while trying to escape from a rather voluptuous woman in clear-spiked heels and a hot pink catsuit.

"I'm so sorry, but . . ." He looked over his shoulder for the lady in pink, and seemed relieved when she was waylaid by a couple of frat-boy types.

I had to laugh. "No worries. So what's your word?"

He dug in his blazer pocket looking for his pad. "Um . . . here we go—*body*." He flexed what appeared to be a decent sized biceps and made a muscle man face. We both laughed.

"Well I'm *some*." We shook hands. "Nice to meet you."

"Finally a match. I was starting to worry I'd been given a bogus word without any matches in the place."

I giggled. It seemed that even in playing this simple game with a room filled with other single people, some still missed the point of just meeting people and having a little fun.

"Sure glad I could do that for you. Now you can say you've had at least one match tonight. My work is done here. Once again, I've saved the planet for all mankind."

He got the joke. "Superman right?" His name was Glen. He was a public school math teacher studying to become a principal and had been encouraged to come to the event. Although he was twenty-nine, he looked like he barely had to shave. As we were about to exchange cell phone numbers, Kay dashed over.

"Excuse me," she said, stepping between Glen and me. "There's someone I want you to meet."

I stepped back next to Glen, gave Kay the hand, and handed Glen my number. He was gracious. "I'll call you," he said walking away.

"Kay, what is wrong with you? Didn't you see I was busy?"

Kay grabbed my arm leading me through the crowd. "Oh later for the little boy. He didn't even look old enough drink. And you need to be circulating, anyway." She spun around like Wonder Woman minus the cape. "How many guys have you met so far?"

"Not counting the senior citizens, one—and you drove him off."

"All right, little Miss Some. It's time for you to go get some of your own, and I have a few matches lined up for you."

Entering the other room my eyes locked onto a man who bore a striking resemblance to Luke. I thought I might be sick. As we approached the group of three men in well-made dark suits, they were all smiles and so was Kay. Luckily it wasn't Luke. She whispered to me, "Now, be nice." I just narrowed my eyes at her.

"Guys this is my friend, Some."

All the guys smiled but the Luke look-alike gave me a wink. Their words—*thing, day,* and *time*—did indeed match mine. The Luke look-alike's word was *time* and his name was Drew. He was a little forward.

"So 'Some,' can I call you . . . some . . . time?" He made a wacky face that made me laugh. "No, I'm serious, I'd like to get together with you."

I just responded we'll see and tried to make sure the group conversation continued. As the group migrated towards the bar, Drew handed me his card.

"Look, take my numbers. I'm a pretty straightforward guy, I'm not really up for the dating game, and I'd like to see you again. You know how to find me." He said goodnight to the other guys and left.

Kay saw him leave and rushed over to me. "What did you *say* to him?"

"Relax. He gave me his numbers and wants to go out. Seemed a bit eager and a little odd, but stranger things have already happened tonight. I'll be back. I'm gonna get some air."

I walked over to the staircase leading down to the lobby. I was ready to go but figured I'd people-watch to give Kay more time to do her thing. While I was standing there and minding my own business, a very tan Ben Kingsley–type walked up beside me.

"So what's your word? No, let me guess—is it *inter*?" As if he knew I wanted to be sure he *wasn't* Ben Kingsley.

I didn't want to play anymore but I tried to be pleasant. "No, it's *some*."

"Oh, that's one of the better ones I've met tonight. Are you a virgin?"

"Excuse me?"

"I mean, is this your first event? I've been coming for the last few years, since my wife left me. It's been good for me. I've been able to keep a study stream of companions, if you know what I mean." He chuckled to himself.

I was grossed out. He was so unctuous I wanted to take a shower. I was *so* ready to go. "So what's *your* word? I don't think you told me."

"It's *side*."

"Well, *side*, I guess we don't match. Have a good night."

As I was heading back inside to find Kay, we bumped into each other.

She gave me a knowing look. "Ready to go, aren't you?"

I smiled and looked at my watch. "Yeah, it's about that time. I don't have to go *home*, but I've got to get out of here."

"Fine, fine. I already have five guys' numbers. That's a large enough sample for a few dates for the next month or so."

Although I'd be treating Kay to Carapan, tonight as a swinging single hadn't been so bad. And then I heard myself think, "Is that how you feel, or are you just kidding yourself?" And all these other questions piled themselves on top: What is this dating thing *really* about? Is it about avoiding commitment until you grow tired of the game? Has it all boiled down to always trying to close a deal, be it getting laid (the transaction) or getting the ring (the transformation)? Does everything have to be about sex, boning, getting in the panties, getting my groove back? And whatever happened to just-plain friendships—you know, enjoying somebody's company? Unfortunately, I didn't have any answers to go along with those questions.

On Wednesday I called Kay to see how her end of the bet was coming along.

"Kay, can you believe that Glen still hasn't called me back? It's already been two days."

"Stop obsessing. If he doesn't call you it doesn't *have* to mean he doesn't want to talk with you. He'll call when he calls. And anyway you clearly have things to do."

"Like what?"

"For starters, how about getting some exercise? You'd be less manic if you burned off some of that excess energy. You'll feel better, sleep better, and look better."

"Hold up—are you trying to say I'm fat?"

Big sigh. "No, I am not *trying* to say anything, except that you need to get a grip. You need to take your life back and stop riding the emotional roller coaster. You take each and every date so seriously. I thought this Friday-night-dating thing was supposed to be about you getting unobsessed and learning to have a good time again, not looking for the *next* obsession. How about working on yourself and working on becoming friends with these boys, instead of looking for Mr. Knight in Shining Armor? You need to slow down, get to know yourself, and get to know who's coming to dinner before offering dessert."

I didn't say a word. Kay just loves the few chances she gets to take the moral high ground with me, and I didn't want to spoil her rare opportunity. Plus she was right. I'd been wanting too much too soon without taking the time to figure out whom I was allowing in my life. I'd been missing the feeling of "couple-dom." I missed being a part of someone's life and sharing my life with someone else. I had identified all those things that allowed someone else in: the last call of the day; the first call of the day; falling asleep and waking up together; nightly and morning rituals—making coffee, listening to NPR; shopping and cooking together; watching favorite TV shows together; calling to share the wins and losses of the work day; working out together; planning weekend activities; sharing news of family and friends. I missed feeling needed by someone else, of sharing the day-to-day with someone, of my being in the world mattering to someone, other than my friends and family.

But disappointment, insecurity, and heartache will make you unnecessarily mean to yourself. Each time I had to forget someone, let go, move on, get over it, I was walling off a part of myself. I'd promise myself next time would be different. I'd incorporate the thing(s) he said, whoever the "he" was, that was not there to create the "us"—the couple-dom. I refused to develop habits or rituals with another man. I would not allow myself or allow another man to become too close.

I'd learned and mastered letting go and didn't want to remember to hold on. It just hurt too much and I didn't want the pain of having to forget all the day-to-day things about being with someone all over again. It was not just about being gun-shy; it was that the risk versus the reward had too many unknown and volatile variables. For once in my life I'd love to know what it feels like not to have any, feel any, or be in the middle of any drama, or confusion.

To quote Lenny Kravitz, I just wanted "to let love rule." This boy/girl thing is just so contrived. Boy and girl meet. They "date" and get to know each other. The families meet. They get engaged and get married. If only it were so simple. So when does the friendship actually happen? I was confused about the whole process again. This was worse than high school, because now everybody—and I mean *everybody*—but me had someone. When did I become the ugly girl at the dance?

Having someone to do things with was just fine with me. No attachment. Isn't that what men do? The pairs or the spares did not need to be fully in my life. My family, friends, work, and things most important to me were off-limits—nothing too deep, too revealing, too personal. It was about having a good time for good time's sake. But even still, in the good time for good time's sake, it's about relating to people, being with people. Impressions, memories, relationships are still developed. I can't control other people, but I can control who and what I allow in my life. Kay was right about that much.

Meeting Glen and Drew just re-ignited my hope that maybe there was someone for me. I got off the phone with Kay and called Drew.

"Hey, I'm glad you finally called. What are you doing Friday night? I have an extra ticket to the Prince concert. You up for it?"

I remembered that he seemed a little forward when we met but between watching *20/20* or going to see Prince, I'll take "The Artist" formerly known as "Prince" any time. We made arrangements to meet. I thought *Later for Glen,* but just as I hung up with Drew, guess who called.

"Hey, I'm sorry I'm just now calling you. I've been swamped and on the West Coast all week. By the time I could call it was too late." I felt like a heel. "I was wondering if you'd like to meet for dinner or something on Friday." He sounded so sweet and worn out, but you snooze, you lose.

"I'd love to but I can't." He didn't need to know I was going to see Prince with someone else, even though Drew and I were just hanging out.

"Oh, well, when can I see you?"

"How about brunch on Saturday."

"Cool. Cool. I'll call you Saturday morning."

Within a matter of moments I'd gone from no dates to two. The concert was great but Drew was another story. Six months ago he broke up with his girlfriend of four years. All night he talked about her. Every song Prince played drove Drew back down memory lane. A woman walked by. He ducked. He thought it was her. Had it not been Prince I might have left, but I focused on the music and I tried to pretend that I was with Max, just hanging out. At the end of the concert Drew was clearly still lamenting his breakup. I'd been there before and would probably be there again but I was in no mood to play relationship-breakup therapist. We parted and I said I'd give him a call. But I didn't.

Glen and I met for brunch at the Pink Teacup, a tiny little soul food place in the West Village. We had a great time. For once someone wasn't tripping on the fact that I didn't come across like a weak wussy woman. I couldn't remember the last time I'd gone out with a brother where he was actually interested and listened to me. We spent the rest of the afternoon running errands—Barnes & Noble, Tower Records, I had to return a sweater to the Gap, he needed to find a comforter cover at Bed Bath & Beyond. We talked and laughed and had a great time until we went to drop off his bags at his apartment in the West Village.

"Like my place?"

"Very nice. You have a great space." I sat on the sofa.

"Did you take a look at the whole place? Did you check out the bedroom?"

"No, but thanks."

"C'mon, let me give you the grand tour." Off down the hallway we went. But his bedroom looked just like every other bedroom in every other pre-war building one-bedroom apartment in New York. "Do you think the duvet cover we bought goes?"

It was blue. The curtains were the same blue. The walls were cream. "Yes, it matches." I headed back to the living room. A few moments later he came back and sat on the sofa next to me.

"What's up with you?" Something was bothering him, and it was clear he wasn't going to be shy about telling me.

"Nothing. What's up with you?"

"Well, you just walked out of my bedroom. You didn't even seem the slightest bit interested in trying out the new duvet."

"Glen, it's not personal, but I'm not interested in getting down."

"Tell me you're not all caught up in that 'I've got to know someone for x number of months and do y number of things with him before I can sleep with him."

"No. That's not it at all."

"Then what? You're single, professional, you've got your

own mind and your own life. You're not a virgin are you? So what are you saving it for? I'm successful."

He should have been careful asking for the truth from a person with little to lose.

"First of all, a woman being self-sufficient has nothing to do with whom she sleeps with, when, or why. Second, we're not really dating. We're just getting to know each other, and whatever your bank account might look like is not going to get me to decide if I should sleep with you. I don't know what kind of woman you've been hanging out with, but I'm not that kind. And what kind of man are you? We're just hanging out and now you're trying to get me to spend the night. For all you know I could have a refrigerator at home filled with men's penises."

"That's disgusting!"

"No, you're disgusting."

I grabbed my packages and left. We never spoke again. So much for a pair and a spare. I'd just have to stick to having only one hole to run into—my own.

20

Getting Specific

My Grandma always said . . .
Give God some time

After the last round of Friday night
disasters I awoke one Sunday morning with a
full-blown headache, crying, and feeling sorry
for myself. I'd just had enough. Having my first
cup of coffee normally helped put things in perspective, but today it only upset my stomach.

I needed some relief. Two deals were closing
this week, so I couldn't take a long weekend,
much less a vacation right now. I didn't want to
go home, either. I wasn't up for the third degree
about why I wasn't dating anyone seriously, or
a sermon from Daddy about working so much

(guess who taught me to be a workaholic), or the lecture on the evils of caffeine and how it was killing my metabolism and making me fat.

It was eleven o'clock Sunday morning. I didn't have the energy for a run or a walk to clear my head, and I wasn't up to meeting anyone for brunch. It had been a while since I'd been to church (okay, nearly nine months), but this seemed as good a morning as any to take my problems to God. Service started at 11:30. I could be pulled together and be there by 11:45, in time to catch a few hymns, write a check, and hear the sermon.

I put on my black Tahari suit, the only one in my closet I could get into comfortably. All the work stress, cocktailing, and dining at midnight had caught up to me, in the form of twenty new pounds. My weekend workouts weren't slowing the growth of my ever-widening hips, or compensating for the damage I did to myself during the week. I hadn't even had a baby yet and I was going to have to subscribe to the Zone. Maybe God *was* trying to tell me something.

As I sat in the pew I wondered what it was all about. What was I missing that I'd kept meeting jerk after jerk? There had to be more to life than working sixteen-hour days, always playing catch-up, putting on the mask to look good and be "normal," fighting the battle of the bulge. All the go-go, rush-rush, run was making me just tired. Sitting in church I sorely wanted God to give me some answers, some purpose, some direction, some relief from this madness that was my life.

I stopped navel-gazing long enough to hear the choir crank up "My Soul's Been Anchored in the Lord." Oh, how tired I was. With each verse I felt the tears building. How did I get here? Where had I gone wrong? What was I doing to make each day, week in and week out, feel like *Groundhog Day*? I thought I'd been doing what I was supposed to do: I was an honest person, I was leading a productive life, I had succeeded and was accomplished by all standards—except in having a meaningful relationship with someone; I hadn't found someone to share my life with. The song finished and I blinked back the tears.

The reverend instructed us each to turn to the neighbor to our right and ask, "Do you know what time it is?" Well, I turned to my neighbor, who happened to have the most beautiful long eyelashes I'd ever seen on a man. His cinnamon-brown complexion and gentle, chocolate brown, almond-shaped eyes startled me. Had he been sitting there the entire service? I had to compose myself. I did not come to church to scope out men—I was here to get right with God.

The reverend continued. "God wants you to be happy. God wants you to be joyful every minute of the day. God wants you to know, to feel, to roll around in love. And do you know how to get there? Do you know? What does Kool Moe Dee ask? Do you know what time it is? Tell me, do you know? Do you know what time it is? Let us turn to the text. What does Jesus say in Luke, chapter 18, verse 27? 'All things are possible with God.' "

"*Now* do you know what time it is? Nah, y'all *still* don't know. Well, I came by here to tell you. You got to go to God to find out what time it is. But y'all gotta look *up,* because y'all too busy looking around at your material things: your house, your car, your gear, your degrees on the wall, your job, your man, your woman, and you looking at what you ain't got. You so busy looking at yourself, and looking at everybody else's stuff, comparing, wondering what's wrong with you, that you missing everything else God has given you. You need to look outside of yourself and look to God to get you through."

Two great organ chords ("doom, doom!"), and the choir sang again.

"Jesus is on the main line, tell him what you want. Jesus is on the main line, tell him what you want. Tell him what you want, tell him what you want, 'cause he's my friend . . .'"

I told God what I wanted—the fine brother sitting next to me. And prayer does work. At the end of the service he gave me a fellowship hug. He smelled good and had supple, well-developed arms and chest.

"Do you worship here often?"

"It's been a minute, but this is my church home."

"I've never seen you here before, but I only joined about nine months ago. Ever been to the youth ministry group on Friday nights?"

Ooh—church on Friday night had never been my idea of a rocking good time. "Uh, no, I haven't." But if he was going to be there, I'd have to work it out.

"Well, I facilitate one of the breakout discussion groups. This Friday we're beginning a new series, 'Being Single and Dating with Christ.' Are you single or dating?"

Did I have that hungry single sista look? Could he tell? I took a deep breath. It was okay; I was in church, and God was with me.

"I am single, and I do date."

"Are you dating anyone seriously?"

"Not really right now."

"Really?" He gave a surprised look. I hate that look—I always think it means *Is it because you're psychotic, or just terminally ill?* "Good—I mean, then you might find someone—I mean, something useful from the series. My name's Bruce. Do you have a card? Here's mine. I'll give you a call about Friday night."

I had to hold back a laugh. God had been trying to tell me something and Mama is always right—church *is* a great place to meet men. Walking home, I did feel better. Maybe there was hope. As I walked in the door my phone was ringing. It was Olga.

"Where have you been all morning? I tried your cell and the voice mail picked up. You have some boy in your house?"

"No, silly—I went to church." I heard her drop something.

"Ohmigod, are you feeling okay? It is that bad? You want me to come over?"

"I'm fine, especially now. I met this fine brother at church."

"You need to be shot. You're such a heathen, going to church to pick up men. I *know* your mama didn't raise you that way."

"It was my mama who *told* me I needed to take my heathen behind to church! Anyway, he invited me to the Friday night youth ministry group."

"Are you serious? You're not going, are you?"

"Of course I am! He's fine, and maybe I'll even get something out of it. Besides, it beats the rest of the nonsense that's been going on. I sure haven't found Prince Charming at a club so maybe I'm due for a little divine intervention. You know, God works in strange and mysterious—"

"Oh, don't be playing with God, or turning out some wholesome church boy. I know you need some Jesus, but don't go becoming a holy roller to catch some man."

I laughed. "Olga, you're on crack. You need to put the pipe down."

"You know men are men whether they are in church or not. And I hate how you get hurt all the time—you always look for the best in people when they're nothing but demon seed."

"Well, you *could* come with me if you're that concerned . . ."

"No thanks. I got a few other things to do on Friday night. But you need to call Kay and invite her ridiculous ass. Have you spoken to her lately?"

"No, what happened now?"

"I'm not telling. I'll let her tell you so you can rip her a new one. I'll surely be glad when your husbands find you two fools."

"As my grandmother used to say, God watches out for babies and fools. I'm not worried."

"That ain't nothing but the truth."

"But how quickly have you forgotten. How many frogs did you have to kiss before Claude? Shall I name names? And when did marriage become the Garden of Eden?"

"Don't get stank. What happened to the Jesus you got this morning?"

"What are you doing home anyway? Aren't you and Mr. Hubby supposed to be going to the Knicks game?"

"He took Max. That's why I called you, anyway. You want to go to Alonzo Adams' opening in Soho? I'm feeling a new piece for the den."

"Who's hosting this party? I'm not up for any drama today."

"Aw, just put on something cute and come on. I'll pick you up by three o'clock. Curl your hair and be ready to go." Click.

This was shaping up to be a decent day after all. I called Kay to see what was going on. Voice mail. I tried her cell and office phones—both voice mail. We'd have to catch up later.

As always, Olga was on time and perfectly manicured. I sighed. *If that's what it's going to take to find a husband, I might as well sign up for the convent. This is as good as it's going to get for right now.*

At the gallery, it was the scene—Sunday afternoon pretense at its best but with decent champagne. Olga found a piece for her den. Mr. Hubby would think twice next time before he gave away Olga's Knicks ticket. And I found the engineer.

I saw him when we walked in but I didn't think I was his type—or he mine for that matter. He was surrounded by a group of women who all could have been on the cover of *Vogue.* I'd learned long ago to develop disdain for what you know you don't have a snowball's chance in hell of getting. After Kurt, I made sure to avoid men who seemed like they even *might* be Barbie-infatuated. He'd be the afternoon's eye candy. He was at least six foot two and statuesque, a Rick Fox look-alike, café-au-lait brown, with wavy, jet black hair. I did my best to ignore him but everywhere Olga and I went throughout the exhibit he seemed to pop up. As Olga gushed over to a piece of art, the engineer strolled up behind us.

"Don't you think the combination of the brush strokes and his use of color and shading creates a unique texture?"

Before I could say anything he chimed in responding to Olga, "You have great eyes and a great eye for detail."

I snickered. Olga blushed.

"I guess your snicker means you don't think so."

"Actually, on the contrary. I'd agree he's created a unique texture in this piece. It draws the viewer's eye to the foreground."

It was his opening line that I was snickering about, but I didn't want to crush him as he made the play for Olga. Even though she was married, Olga never minded a little extra attention. And marriage hadn't made her homely—she looked better now than she did when she was single. Having another income to spend had done wonders for her wardrobe. She'd upgraded to having a seamstress.

"It's always great to meet people who actually come to appreciate an artist's work, and not to pick up men."

I snickered again. Presumptuous fellow. Olga nudged me with her prized Prada bag, flashing her six-carat diamond engagement ring *and* her five-carat diamond-and-sapphire eternity band by placing her hand over her ample bosom. Smiling smugly and in her most ladylike tone, she said, "I'm (ahem), I'm married." She hesitated for a second, almost as if she had been debating whether or not to say so.

"Really? And what about you, Miss Snicker?"

"Oh, I'm just single. Still trolling for the likes of you." I excused myself and headed for the bathroom. I'd had about as much pretension and conceit as I could take in one conversation. When I returned from the bathroom Olga and her new friend were chatting away.

"This is Dale. He's Reverend Gerald's cousin. You remember Reverend Gerald from our wedding? He married us. Dale's a fascinating man. He's also an artist—he paints watercolors."

I mustered a disdainful, "Nice to meet you."

"Olga tells me you have an affinity for African-American art, especially William Johnson. He's one of my favorites, too. Do you have any of his pieces?"

"Yes."

Olga rolled her eyes. "You can be so modest. She actually has several."

I gave Olga the evil eye.

"It's nice meeting you Dale, but it's time for me and Olga to go."

"Ladies, I don't want to hold you up. But a close friend is having an opening a week from Friday. Would you two like to join me at the reception?"

"Of course we would." Olga grinned, and whipped out her handheld to take down the details. She was shameless at times.

"Will you be able to make it? Hopefully, I'll see you there." It never ceases to amaze me. Treat them mean and they always like it.

Olga and I took advantage of the beautiful day for a Soho stroll. "Now what's wrong with him?" He's gorgeous and he's a biochemical engineer with a Ph.D. from MIT."

"He's also pretentious, and conceited, in case you hadn't noticed, so give me a break. I'll pass."

"He was checking you out and I think he was digging that you weren't sweating him. *That's* the type of man you should be dating. Successful, cultured, and fine." She added in a singsong, "He could be husband material."

I had a headache now and *The Sopranos* was coming on at eight o'clock and I needed to get home. The work week passed at a dizzying pace.

MONDAY: Reading and editing documents, conference calls.

TUESDAY MORNING: Take a 5:40 A.M. flight to Denver.

WEDNESDAY EVENING: Take flight back to New York.

THURSDAY: An all-day meeting that began at 8:30 A.M.

By the time Bruce, the cutie I'd met in church, called Friday morning, I could only think about spending a quiet Friday evening at Kay's with Max and Olga, watching movies and eating Chinese.

"Hi, it's Bruce from church."

"Hey, how are you?"

In the background I could hear a flurry of activity, telephones ringing, cursing, and shouting. Shouting into the telephone, "Thanks for asking! I'm okay! I just wanted to remind you about tonight's youth ministry group! Will you be able to make it? It starts at 7:30 in the church study."

I shouted back. "I'll do my best."

We laughed at the silliness of the shouting. "Great, I'll see you there!"

When I arrived at 7:45 the room was filled with both men and women. Most looked to be between the ages of twenty-five and forty, both casual and suit-clad, all intensely focused on Bruce's calm, soothing, yet authoritarian voice.

"Looking for a mate in this confusing world takes something. And that something isn't a large wad of cash, an expensive car or big breasts, long hair, or a shapely figure. We have to be vigilant of all the temptations and distractions that will have us put everything but God first in our lives. God must be first in our lives—to guide us. We have to pray exactly in the moment of temptation when we're about to engage in sin."

Now that made some sense, but then he lost me.

"God has given both men and women roles to fulfill—man to provide and woman to support, to take care of her man, and the home." Was I in *The Twilight Zone*? Had I stepped through some portal and been transported back to the 1950s?

Looking around, both men and women were nodding their heads in agreement. He was tripping. They were tripping. Most folks I know *have* to work for a living, and it isn't about providing or supporting—it's about surviving. Most folks don't have the luxury to play out some antiquated notion of men do this and women do that. And anyway, most of us can't afford to be so narrowly defined when this economy demands everyone to work to make ends meet.

"Okay, let's break up into groups of five and discuss God's roles for men and women, and strategies for dating and identifying a truly Christian mate."

I'd come to the group in hopes of finding an alternative perspective, and now it just seemed to be another variation on the same theme. But since this was my Friday night date, I joined one of the groups. I couldn't believe that in this day and age well-educated folks were still walking around holding on to such outdated notions. Had I missed something? We counted off in fives and moved towards our appointed places in the room. Bruce joined the group but before everyone could even arrange their chairs in a circle he upped the ante, spewing venom about the evils of women.

"Women don't know their place. If women weren't running around trying to be so independent, we'd all be married by now. If a woman gets a job making more than $60,000, she's just out for herself. Career women are worse than men—just want to use up all you got. And they're easy. That's why more men don't respect women. To be so independent, women fall for the same ole' same ole'. If a man flatters you, shows the slightest bit of interest, takes you to dinner at a decent restaurant, pays you a few compliments, and God forbid calls you a few times, you're ready to bed him down. And then you get mad when he disappears after the wham-bam-thank-you-ma'am. And *then*, when he doesn't return your calls, you just call, call and call, harassing him. And *then* you want to slap a restraining order on him when he tells you if you call again he'll have you arrested for stalking him!"

I had heard enough. I excused myself and headed for the bathroom but kept walking out the door. Bruce wasn't the godsend I thought, but he had given me a few things to think about. I'd keep praying, but it was clear that I needed to be a little more specific.

21

House Calls

My Grandma always said . . .
Start out like you can hold out

I continued to go to church on Sundays, and saw Bruce faithfully recruiting young members to attend the Friday night singles group. He clearly needed some Jesus *and* therapy to work through his bitterness and find some forgiveness. I knew I had my share of issues to work through too, but I wasn't interested in his brand of group therapy.

This Friday I would attend the exhibit with Olga. I hated to admit it, but Dale was cute, and Pretty-Ricky Negroes always reek of trouble. I was no longer looking for the exception to the rule. I just suspected he would be like the rest—playing and gaming. Olga and I met after work at Panache to have dinner before heading to the gallery on Greene Street.

"I need a drink."

"Olga, is it that bad?"

"Got a minute? Let me tell you a story."

"I'm listening."

"Well, you know Claude and I haven't been in the best space for more than a minute. He's been moody and distant. I thought it was just work, his traveling, and simply settling into married life. And you know I've had my own stuff going on."

"What stuff?"

"Well, this is hard to talk about. Monday I went for my annual GYN checkup and they found cysts on my ovaries. They're about the size of oranges. They aren't sure if they are cancerous but I'll have to have surgery. I may not be able to have children."

"Oh, no!"

Olga waved her hand to stop me. "That's not the bad part."

"Oh, Olga!" I grabbed her hand, and she started crying.

"I've been trying to keep it together, but everything's falling apart. I'm taking a month off from work to just focus on getting healthy. The office has been really supportive, and the doctors have been great." Olga collected herself when the waiter arrived to take our orders. "I'll have a Johnnie Walker Black straight up."

"You don't drink hard liquor. You sure you want that?"

"Back off of me. I'm sorry, but it *may* calm my nerves."

"No, I'm sorry. Sista, tell me what I can do."

The tears started again. "And that Claude. Can you believe what he said to me? The other night we were in bed, he kissed my stomach and said, 'Guess I might as well start saying good-bye.' I was so mortified I had to get up and go sleep in the den. He can't fathom how hard this is for me. This isn't a joke—this is my body! The next morning he told me to think of the bright side. He said losing my ovaries would be better than my losing a breast. He said he didn't know whether he'd be able to deal with my having a fake breast."

"Bastard!"

"It's not his body being cut up and cut off. He's not the person I married. I can't even stand being in the same room with him now. I don't think I can get past this. And what if I *do* have to have my ovaries removed? What stupid-ass thing will he say then? It's enough for me to deal with this. I just don't have the energy to deal with *him* dealing with me. He's supposed to be the love of my life, my best friend, and my rock in times like this. I swear, I'm thinking about moving out."

By now she was crying into her plate. I hugged her, and she quietly sobbed into my shoulder. As for Claude, all I could think was *Rat Bastard*. He had never struck me as the touchy-feely type, but this was just downright mean. What happened to "in sickness and in health"? I guess it didn't mention anything about compassion and kindness. Their courtship and engagement had been six months and they married a year to the day from their first date. They'd met at a fundraiser where he was auctioned off. Olga paid nearly a thousand dollars for an evening out with him. He was handsome, successful, and funny. They'd hit it off and began a whirlwind courtship. He traveled a lot but spent all his free time with her when he was in town. Within three months they'd met the parents and started talking about marriage. Olga was the picture of prenuptial happiness. At thirty-two she had felt like this was as good as it was going to get and she didn't want to hear anyone's suggestion that she take another year or so getting to know him. The grass is always greener on the other side until the drought comes.

"Let's get out of here. Do you want to go home?"

"Not on your life. We're going to the exhibit. Let me fix my face. I can't stop living my life because my body and my marriage are falling apart."

"Have you guys thought about counseling?"

"He says that's for people with problems. He doesn't see my health issues and his being an asshole as problems. Not *his* problem, anyway."

"What about therapy for you?"

"Way ahead of you. I have an appointment next week. I've come too far to let him and whatever is going on with my body make me someone I don't want to be. I'm going to live with or without him but I'm not going to be miserable anymore. Fuck him and fuck this cancer. I don't want to talk about this anymore right now. I want to just go out, have a good time tonight, and if no more than for a few hours forget about Claude and my ovaries. It's Friday night and we have an exhibit to go see. Just because my life is falling apart and I'm miserable doesn't mean that everyone around me should be falling apart and miserable, too. It's clearly not over for all of us. And anyway that cutie Dale is going to be there, and he's probably waiting at the door for you. Let's go!" We talked for a few more minutes and then walked to the gallery, Olga's spirits rising the more we walked and talked.

And she was right—Dale *was* standing near the front of the gallery when we arrived.

"What a pleasant surprise—two of my favorite women!"

He looked so happy I was sure it must be fake. "You just met us two weeks ago."

He laughed. "Well, it's great to see you, too."

"Dale, pay her no mind. I'm still working on her social skills."

"Come on in and enjoy the art. The bar and hors d'oeuvres are to your left. Let me show you around and introduce you to the artist."

As we walked through the exhibit and Dale chatted me and Olga up, I couldn't shake my dinner conversation with her. Is that what marriage has to offer? You think you've found someone who will be your life mate and be there through thick and thin, but when the going gets tough he just becomes an asshole? As much I'd been wishing on a star and trying to be open even after all my dating experiences, Olga's situation made me think that the single life does have its advantages. When fate throws a curveball, I may not have a special someone to provide comfort and kindness, but my friends and family never waver. They love me unconditionally and lend me the support I need. The thought of being in a relationship/marriage, having something of this magnitude happen, and *not* having my significant other "be there" gave me a strange comfort in being single. I didn't know what I was going to do, but I'd rather figure out how to be happy alone than have someone like Claude.

Dale tapped me on the shoulder. "You seem to have just left us. You look like you have a lot on your mind. You know, I'm a great listener."

I gave him a weak smile. "Sorry. That happens sometimes. But thanks for the offer."

"You come across like a macho woman, but when you're

gazing into space just then, I could see that you have a feeling and compassionate side."

I was not in the mood for the pretend thoughtful, sensitive male routine. I glanced over my shoulder to see Olga, standing nose to nose with the artist looking like they were about to swap spit. "Excuse me for a moment."

"Yeah, it looks like Olga may have had a few too many and I'd hate to be the one to break it to her, but he's married, too."

Olga was a lightweight. She usually never drank anything stronger than champagne. The Johnnie Walker Black and the emotional stress had caught up with her. I'd only left her for about five minutes.

"There you are. You guys met when we came in." She was giggling, clearly tipsy. "Isn't he adorable? And look at this." She extended her arm toward the wall, almost touching the painting and knocking the glass out of my hand. "He's a genius, see the color, the expression, the compassion, and the warmth. I'm taking this home." She whispered in my ear audibly, "And maybe him, too!"

"Time to go."

"Oh, come on. I'm just having a little fun and he's adorable. But the painting, I want the painting." They exchanged cards, and I guided Olga by the forearm toward the door where Dale was standing.

"Thanks for inviting us, but it's about that time."

"I'm sorry you have to leave so soon. I don't mean to be forward but could I interest you in cocktails or dinner sometime?"

I took a deep breath. "Here's my card. But we really have to go." Olga was now talking to everyone who walked by about how wonderful the exhibit was. What a night. I took a cab with Olga to make sure she got home and then headed back to my place. Looking at his card I thought, *well I've dated worse. A biochemical engineer, you never know . . .*

He did call and we did go out the following Friday. We had dinner at the 12th Street Café in Park Slope. He was funny, thoughtful and a total gentleman. He told great funny stories about the fine line between brilliance and insanity that gets crossed regularly when you're working in a lab, and he was a great listener. Before we knew it, it was nearly 2:00 A.M. and we were the last people in the restaurant.

"Wow, I guess it's about that time. I can't believe I'm actually saying this, but time really *does* fly when you're having fun."

Dale smiled, "I guess that means we'll have to get together again."

This was almost too good to be true. It had been a while since I'd gone out with a guy who acted like he had some home training, and was truly interested in spending time with me, not just getting into my pants. He'd asked me out again even before our date had really ended. In the car on the way to my house there wasn't any sexual overtures or innuendo, no trying to feel me up or out as to whether he would be invited in to spend the night. He gave me a kiss on the cheek and said goodnight. I went to sleep pretty pleased with the evening. It had been a good Friday night.

He called Saturday afternoon.

"I wanted to say thanks again for last night. I really enjoyed dinner with you. Now be honest with me—will I sound overeager if I ask to get together again this week?

"No . . ." He had to sense my smiling through the phone. "Not in the least. I had a great time, too, and I'd love to get together again. Problem is, I'm traveling most of the week, but I'm back on Thursday."

"Aw . . ." He sounded slightly disappointed, but in a charming way. "So Friday night then?"

"Sure. Let's talk on Friday."

By the time I returned to the city Thursday evening, I had caught a nasty cold. Feeling like a Mack truck had hit me, I decided to stay home on Friday. A long weekend resting indoors might help me kick my cold. He called mid-afternoon.

"I called your office. They said you were home sick. Why didn't you call me?"

"I figured I'd talk to you this evening."

"I'm off in an hour, and I'll be right over. What do you need?"

"You don't have to do that. I'm just sleeping and you don't have time to catch my cold."

"I'm on my way. Consider it a house call. I'm surrounded by more hazardous materials than your puny germs all day long." He arrived an hour later with flowers and groceries. "Yeah you've got a cold but I've got a cure." He made me homemade chicken noodle soup, and raw ginger tea, with onion, cayenne pepper, honey, lemon, and a shot of whiskey. The tea was awful.

"Oh! This is horrible! Did they teach you this at MIT?"

"No, my grandmother did, and I bet you a backrub that you're going to feel better in the morning."

"You're on!"

Friday evening I did begin to feel a bit better—for a while. We played Scrabble and cards until my fever returned. "Oh, I don't feel too good."

He took my temperature, gave me another round of vitamins and cold medicine, and put me to bed. I was asleep in minutes and awoke the next morning to the smell of breakfast cooking. He had slept on the sofa.

He brought me breakfast in bed, "You're feeling better, and now—you've got to feed that cold." I was feeling better, but it wasn't solely from the chicken soup and medicine. It had been a long while since anyone had shown me any real TLC or since I'd let anyone even try. I'd almost forgotten how heartwarming TLC could be.

That day we talked, cooked, played board games, watched movies, napped together off and on until my hormones got the better of me. While we cuddled on the sofa he said he'd like to see me exclusively. Having been through the dating wringer, I was still wary. Could it be this simple? Lying next to him, snotty nose and all, I couldn't believe that my getting sick helped me see that maybe he really was interested in me. I was slightly overcome by gratitude and one thing led to another.

The first time, I thought it was nerves, over-excitement, the newness of it all.

The second time, later that evening, I thought it was maybe because he'd had too much wine with dinner. He did drink most of the bottle.

The third time in the middle of the night, I began to wonder if it was me. Was I too aggressive? Was there too much foreplay? We resorted to heavy petting, and I felt like I was back in prep school, making out on the lower soccer field.

The fourth time we tried, I wondered if he had a physical or mental block. He got up, showered, and went to the kitchen to make breakfast. I always thought that no sex was better than bad sex, but I liked everything else about him—

everything! He was so smart and warm and fun and caring. As I changed the sheets I found myself thinking, *Maybe a sexless relationship is doable.* As teenagers we'd had relationships without sex. But there is something about once you've had it it's hard to go back, like coffee without cream and sugar. Oh, who was I lying to? All the breakfasts in bed and Scrabble games in the world wouldn't cut it, a woman has her needs. At breakfast he brought it up.

"I've, um, had this, um . . . problem before. I thought it would be different this time. You know I'm crazy about you and I want to know you in the biblical sense, but all those years of Catholic school and those sermons about burning in hell for fornication pop into my head, every time we're about to go there."

"I see." I'd had nine years of Catholic school and my libido was the least of my troubles, but all right. "Have you ever considered talking with someone about it?"

"I am—you."

"I mean professionally."

"Well, no. But I was thinking I could have my doctor write me a prescription for Viagra."

"Dude, you're not sixty. Why don't you get a physical and *talk* with your doctor about it?"

"I'm not going to a doctor or a shrink to fix my dick. Maybe we should just get married and then it wouldn't be fornication and it might work."

I laughed, "Don't you think that's a bit drastic?"

"No. You know I really want to please you. We have a great time together and get along. We're not getting any younger and we'd make out pretty well. Think about it."

I didn't need to think about. If this was his problem-solving tool kit, no way was I signing up for the long haul. My grandmother always said, "Whatever you don't like about them before you marry will only get worse afterward, so be sure it's something you could live with for a lifetime." The TLC had warmed my heart, but the thought of a sexless marriage chilled it like January.

22

HIV . . . Who Makes That?

My Grandma always said . . .
Do you think I was born yesterday? Do I have
two O's for eyes and a F and L on each
side of my head that spells fool?

After the engineer, my libido took
a nosedive. I'd had about enough of the dating
thing. But Josh called one Tuesday evening as I
walked in the door from a quick day-trip to
Chicago. I'd been up since 5:30 A.M. and the
last thing I really wanted to do was chat with a
slightly boring man. I'd met him at the tennis
court while Kay and I waited for a court. He
lived in the neighborhood and owned his own
consulting firm. He was balding, probably in
his mid-forties and in great shape. We'd spoken
on the phone a few times but I didn't feel any

sparks. I'd occasionally see him on my way to work or while running errands in the neighbor, and I always kept the conversation short.

HE: Hi, it's Josh. I saw you the other morning but you looked like you were in a hurry so I didn't want to bother you. I was wondering if you'd like to play tennis this weekend, or maybe meet for drinks or something on Friday. I hadn't seen you around the neighborhood in a while and thought it would be nice to catch up with you.

ME: Hey, I just walked in the door. Let me give you a call back tomorrow.

I debated whether to call him back or blow him off. The last thing I wanted was some man stalking me in my very own neighborhood. Home was still my sanctuary. I finally called him back Thursday and we arranged to play tennis Friday evening. I needed some exercise but I was not prepared to play with him. He had a very fast and hard serve, and I lost in straight sets. He ran me ragged—I needed to work out more. He invited me to dinner but I was too exhausted and went home to crash.

He called again the following Tuesday and we decided to play again on Friday. "I guess you like winning in straight sets."

He chuckled. "I don't mind playing with you. You've got a little bit of game, and playing with you helps me work on my focus and it's interesting to watch you."

"Oh, you mean my Charlie Brown moves?"

"That's not exactly what I was talking about, but let me not cross the line." Friday evening came, and I actually won two sets. I'd be a little prouder if I didn't strongly suspect he'd *let* me win. Afterwards we decided to grab dinner.

"Why don't you come to my house after you shower and change. I'll make you dinner and maybe we can check out A Table for dessert." I was feeling pretty comfortable with him, and so I went. My comfort was short-lived. When I walked into his apartment the lights were low, candles were everywhere, and Sade was playing. This was not what I had in mind, but the aroma of lamb and stuffed mushrooms and the bright lights in the kitchen where he was working away eased my misgivings. As he prepared dinner, we talked about dating and relationships. He'd been divorced twice before he was thirty-five. He would be turning forty the following month and still had hopes that he'd meet "his person." The first marriage of ten years had ended when he found out his wife was having an affair. The second marriage had ended after his wife, whom he'd met while on vacation in Prague, got her green card. He said that since then he'd just focused on building his business, staying in shape, and dating occasionally but casually.

We had to turn the lights up so we could see our plates and he changed the music from Sade to Lee Morgan. Over dinner we had a good time comparing ridiculous dating stories. Afterwards we played some more music, drank some more wine, and chatted. Next we found ourselves singing along and doing old dances. Then at some point the music changed and we were slow dancing. I was thinking how nice it felt to be held close. Then the dancing stopped and he leaned down and kissed me. It was a perfect kiss—moist but not too sloppy, firm without trying to break my teeth. After we kissed for what seemed like hours we ended up on the sofa and my senses returned in a flash. I sat up to rearrange my clothes.

"Hold up, Josh. Time out."

"Aw, come on. What's the deal?"

"I don't know you."

"We're both consenting adults. I just want to be with you. No drama."

Was I holding out? Why exactly was I keeping my clothes on and legs closed? It had been more than a minute since I'd had any decent sex, and I am an adult, right?

I relaxed a little. "Okay, when was the last time you visited the doctor?"

"College."

End of relaxation. "You mean to tell me that you haven't had a checkup since then?"

"Look, I'm a healthy, virile man, and I'm in great shape."

"That not what I'm asking. Have you had unprotected sex?"

He started laughing, but I don't think he thought it was funny, and I know I didn't. "Be for real. Shit happens. Yes, on occasion I've gone out in the rain without a raincoat, but it wasn't acid rain. I'm careful, and I'm selective. Every woman I've ever slept with is clean."

"How did you know? How can you tell?"

"They just are," he said, sounding indignant that I might even suggest otherwise. "You sure know how to kill a hard-on. Damn!"

"Sorry, but I love me just a little too much to die from something I could have easily avoided."

"What are you talking about? Penicillin cures everything."

"Since when? Herpes and AIDS are incurable, my friend." A thought hit me like a brick. "You've never had an HIV test, have you?"

"HIV? The record store?"

I looked for a hint of a smile. He had to be kidding. "No, that's HMV. HIV is a sexually transmitted disease. It can turn into the AIDS virus. Maybe you've heard it mentioned once or twice in the past fifteen years?!?"

"Yeah, I've heard about AIDS, thank you, but I'm not exactly losing sleep over it. I'm not a drug addict, and I'm not promiscuous. Like I told you, I've always been highly selective."

He was just ignorant. "Meaning you have extrasensory equipment that goes off when someone has the cooties? You're ridiculous. I'm sorry, but there's no room in the inn."

"All right, look, I've got a box of condoms. I'll wear two!"

"Do you think I'm that hard up? Do I look stupid? That's only half the point. Have you ever asked the people you slept with about *their* sexual habits, *their* drug use, or whether *they've* been tested?

"Oh come on. I don't want to be up in their business like that. I just want to have sex. Otherwise I'd be thinking the whole time about all the other guys they've slept with, and that's just nasty. I'd never get laid again."

"Actually, what's nasty is that you have no clue about people's sexual histories and you're sticking your thing inside them on a wing and a prayer. You're lucky that you haven't contracted something. Do you have any idea how many people, especially women of color, are dying from AIDS every year? We're the fastest growing percentage of the population dying from AIDS. And we're not all intravenous drug users or sleeping with bisexual men. A lot of us are just gullible enough to believe a man when he says, 'It's cool baby, I'm clean'!"

He threw up his hands. "What do you want me to say? All

right, last year I caught a cold from a woman I was dating. Y'know, I didn't make you dinner to get a public service announcement. I could have just watched PBS."

"Well, if you *did* watch PBS you might know the difference between HIV and HMV. I've got to go. I'm out of here." I grabbed my bag and headed out the door, grateful to the little impulse that made me break the mood.

"Keep living"

23

Time Challenged a.k.a. CPT (Committed People Tripping)

My Grandma always said . . .
What do you want with
someone else's junk?

Damn it's nearly 7:00 P.M. and I'm just getting off the train, and rushing into Pathmark to get dinner fixings for Olga, Kay, and Max. We've all been having a trying time so we decided to get together for dinner at my house. I decided to cook, Kay would bring dessert, Olga videos, and Max wine. Rushing through the vegetable section trying to remember what was in the fridge and what I needed to pick up, my train of thought was interrupted:

"Excuse me, can you tell me what time it is?"

Time for you to get a watch—I thought but didn't say it, "ten after seven."

"Thanks."

"You're welcome." Going on about my business, Mama was right. You've got to have a grocery list in order not to forget what you're in the store for. Now what else was I forgetting: apples, bread, pasta, sauce, onions, yellow peppers. Peas—that is what I needed. But of course there he was again, the watchless man in the frozen food section. I wasn't paying him any attention when he asked me the time again. I was too busy trying to remember what I needed to make dinner in a rush. He wasn't really my type. He couldn't have been taller than five foot six, overdeveloped upper body, clean-shaven head, with a goatee, glasses, and a million-dollar smile; on second glance, he was workable.

"Looks like you're about to prepare a feast." He was looking in my shopping cart. He held one of those small hand baskets used in the express line. "It's another microwaved dinner night for me." I gave him a grimace and kept looking for the Birds Eye sweet peas. "So you're making dinner for your boyfriend or your husband?" I ignored his question. Was he fishing for an invite? He continued, "I'm Solomon."

"Nice to meet you." I grabbed my frozen peas and headed for the checkout line. Olga, Kay, and Max would be ringing my buzzer in less than an hour and I wasn't in the mood for any jokes about my lateness. He followed me to the check out line. "I don't mean to bother you but I know I've seen you somewhere before and I'm trying to place your face."

Oh brother, I thought. Here we go again. Wasn't that one of the oldest lines in the book? But he kept going.

"Do you work downtown or live in the neighborhood?" I

nodded. "That's it. Now I remember. I saw you in the Au Bon Pain on Whitehall Street. You work in the building next door, don't you?"

You would have thought he hit Lotto. "That's it! That's where I've seen you! I work in One State Street Plaza. We should meet for lunch sometime." Luckily it was my turn at the register and I gave the cashier my full attention. As I hoisted my bags on my shoulder, he handed me his card.

"Give me a call. Let's do lunch sometime."

With my free hand I shoved the card into my pocket making a beeline toward the door. I wanted to get as far away as fast as I could just in case he decided to follow me.

I hadn't thought anymore about the annoying encounter but once you meet someone in New York you run into them everywhere. Seven days later I was waiting for my Arizona chicken in Au Bon Pain when in walked Solomon. I turned my back hoping he wouldn't recognize me, but no such luck.

"Hey. Good seeing you again. How'd your dinner turn out last Friday?"

"Fine. And yours?"

"Delicious. Are you staying for lunch?"

"No. I've got to get back."

"Maybe some other time." He looked like a kicked puppy. Then I noticed the wedding band on his left hand. What a nerve.

"So how long have you been married?" I thought that would cool his heels.

He nervously twisted the band but perked up. "Oh, . . . um about a year."

"So does you wife know that you're asking women on dates?"

He laughed nervously." Oh come on. Just because you get married doesn't mean you stop looking at other people. Anyway, lunch is harmless."

"Thanks, but I really have to go now."

"I guess I'll see you around."

"I don't think so." I headed out the side door. What nerve! Asking young, single women to lunch. But every time I turned around Solomon showed up, on the train, at the deli, near the office, in the cleaners, and at the video store. It seemed like we were on the same schedule. I'd politely say hello and keep moving. But one Friday afternoon I was going over documents while having a late lunch at Au Bon Pain, when Solomon walked in. I'd reach the next level of hazing in the office and had my ass kicked all morning. It seemed that everything I said and did was wrong and initiated a tongue-lashing as well as more work. It would be another working weekend.

He waved and I continued reading, hoping he'd get his coffee and move on, instead he came over and sat down. "Eating and working is bad for your digestion. You'll get an ulcer."

"Thanks I'll keep that in mind." I took another bite out of my sandwich and turned the page.

"How've you been? You look tired and stressed."

I was tired on more levels than he could imagine. Work was grueling and it felt like each time I thought I was getting a handle on either the amount or subject matter of my work the rules of the game changed. I was struggling to keep up while keeping my cool and having my ass handed to me daily. The sense of balance I used to feel was gone. I didn't have time to go to the gym, see friends, or do anything I enjoyed, for that matter. Work had taken over my life. And I'd let it.

And I told him as much. He sat listening, only occasionally

interjecting his perspective. After I poured it all out I felt better.

And so it began. We'd meet for lunch and talk. Then after a while we started having dinners too. We'd just talk about what was going on in our lives—work, my dating, and his marriage. Being fifteen years my senior, he gave me a perspective I greatly appreciated. We'd become friends and began spending our free time together. Our conversations helped me feel more balanced. I began exercising again, found more time to spend with friends and family, went to church on Sundays, prayed daily, read spiritually enriching materials, wrote in my journal, and spent quality time alone. I even enjoyed going to work again. There was no doubt that his friendship made my life feel fuller. But although it seemed harmless, we'd unknowingly created a relationship, one that consisted of sharing our deepest thoughts and feelings. And I knew I looked forward to our outings and conversations as much as he did.

We met for cocktails one Friday night and ended up at Eugene's. We danced, talked and laughed until nearly 3:00 A.M. It was so much fun, and I was so relaxed I didn't want the night to end.

But Saturday morning I wasn't nearly so happy. I woke up feeling anxious and guilty. This would not, could not, carry over into the rest of our lives. Kissing him had blurred the line of our friendship and in the light of day I saw it for the poor choice it was. We were playing in "Never Never Land" and not reality. We'd never be able to explore a "real" relationship. And even if by some chance he decided to divorce his wife would I really want to be with him? I'd certainly never be able to fully trust him.

Then the phone rang. It was Olga. She was crying.

"He didn't come home until five A.M. and when he did he asked me for a divorce. He's met someone else and says he's in love. They've been seeing each other for almost a year. How could he do this to me? How could he do this to us? He said he'd been planning to tell me since before the operation. Like he was so considerate when I was sick. He's moving out today. Fuck him."

Olga and I had brunch, manicures and pedicures, walked around Park Slope, and bought candles and flowers. I felt like such a hypocrite, comforting Olga while I'd been out with someone else's husband the night before. As we ordered mochas in Cousin Johns, Solomon called.

"Are you up for dinner tonight?"

"No. I'll have to pass."

"What's tomorrow look like?"

"Call me in the morning." I hung up.

Olga had stopped counting sugar packets and looked at me.

"Who was that? The mystery man? Kay and I were discussing how incognito you've been about this new one. When are we going to meet him?"

"Never." I shrugged my shoulders and changed the subject. "You want to go to the movies?"

After going through all the listings—too sad, too deep, seen it already, not worth $9.50—we went to Blockbuster. It would be a funny triple feature—*The Original Kings of Comedy*, *The Queens of Comedy* and *Chris Rock Live*—with takeout Chinese. Olga was asleep on the sofa before the first video finished. I, on the other hand, couldn't sleep for thinking about how I was going to deal with Solomon.

I hadn't promised, in front of God, to forsake all others—*he* had. But I felt as guilty as I thought he should, and these were our options:

His:
1. Leave me alone;
2. Divorce the wife he was cheating on;
3. Go to relationship counseling or individual therapy and address the issues in his marriage; or

Mine:
1. Leave him alone;
2. Leave him alone; and
3. Leave him alone.

I didn't sleep at all that night. Here I had dated all these men, seen so much, felt so much, understood so much and yet understood nothing at the same time. It felt like all the work I'd done to pull myself out of my depression was undone. I was officially miserable again and I'd done it to myself. Thinking about entering the singles' scene of barhopping only made me feel worse. There had to be something else and this clearly wasn't it.

Solomon didn't call on Sunday and I had avoided his calls during the week. It was just as well. Olga and Claude had begun making arrangements to separate and my daily chats with Olga only made me feel worse about talking to Solomon. Finally, Claude moved out and Olga planned a two-week vacation to Italy alone.

Friday afternoon I picked up my phone without looking at the caller ID. It was Solomon.

"What you up to tonight? You wanna grab dinner and a movie?"

"No. We need to talk." I said grimly.

"Okay, what have I done now? I figured you were angry about something. You've been screening your calls all week."

I took a deep breath and closed my eyes, "Look, I'm not angry with you. But I'm really pissed off at myself. We can't see each other anymore." There I'd said it. But it felt like being told someone had died. Then the tears started. I knew I was doing the right thing, but it felt terrible.

He was silent for a moment. "I know it's been hard for you. You really want to be in a real relationship and I can't give you that. I'm not interested in leaving my wife. I love her. But I also care a great deal about you, and I really enjoy the time we spend together. I knew we'd eventually need to do this. I just didn't think it would be this soon." He took a deep breath. "I'm gonna miss you."

And just like that it was all over. I was miserable and crying as I headed home. I needed some time alone to think. In fact, that was the very thing I needed, time. I'd been out so much over the past year that I'd forgotten how to just be happy alone with me. And even if I didn't have all the answers yet, I knew there was more to life than what Solomon was offering. After all, as my grandmother used to say, "What do I need with someone else's junk?"

24

The Friend Zone

My Grandma always said . . .
Some things you better keep special

I was staring at my computer screen daydreaming. I missed having someone in my life. I missed the excitement of having shared a night and a morning together hugging and laughing at silly jokes. I craved intimacy, the closeness of lying on another person's chest, hearing his heart beating, of being held by someone who wants me. Me and no one else. My craving turned into a dull ache. My phone rang; it was Max. "What are you doing Friday night?"

"It's only Wednesday. I don't know yet."

"I've got to go to a work formal on Friday. You want to go?"

"You mean to tell me Mr. Casanova doesn't have a date lined up?"

"I'm tired of all the nonsense."

"What happen to Angelica?"

"Too clingy, too needy."

"Pat?"

"Went back to her ex."

"Deloise?"

"Too busy, too bossy."

"Diane?"

"She's a nighthawk. I can't take her out in public."

"Alice?"

"I'd be afraid to leave her alone. If I went to the bathroom she might be bumping and grinding with my boss."

"All right. So what time should I be ready?"

"Can you get off the plantation by six?"

"I'll do my best."

I went for the sexy but conservative look, cocktail length black dress with a black beaded bolero jacket. My bag, shoes, and attitude would have to make the outfit. We sat at a table with his boss, two clients and their wives. After introductions Max went to the bathroom and his boss leaned over, "Max told us you'd be coming. You know he talks about you all the time."

We were so comfortable with each other that people often took us for a couple. And his mother had trained him well. He pulled out my chair, fetched me a drink, included me in the conversation. He even asked me to dance when the swing band started playing. During the slow dance he held me like a woman, not one of his "boys." I could feel his breath on my neck, smell his cologne, and feel the warmth of his embrace. "You look great tonight. The gang really digs you." I don't think he'd ever paid me a compliment like that before. "See I knew you'd be the right one to come with me. It's a shame we're 'boys'—you got eighty percent of my checklist." Now what was that supposed to mean? We were having such a good time that I didn't say a word, and just kept dancing. On the car ride home he fell asleep in my lap. I looked down and realized he was really cute. When we got to my place Max decided he was too tired to go all the way home and decided to crash at my place.

Before I could finish washing my face and brushing my teeth, Max was snoring. I turned off the light and climbed into bed. Around 6:00 A.M. I woke up to find Max's arm wrapped around me and his body snuggled against my backside. For a moment I thought about waking him up, but then I thought, "We're friends and it didn't mean anything. Right?" We were each other's surrogate companion when pickings were slim. We were buddies. We gave each other dating advice. He'd even seen me cry. We knew each other's families. But I couldn't fall back to sleep. Maybe after all this time Max was the one and I'd been too blind to see it. We were totally compatible, he was cute and . . . but before I could finish I'd dozed off again, dreaming that Max was proposing to me.

"Wake up! No wonder guys trip on you. You talk in your sleep." I jumped up and hit him with a pillow, and it was on. Feathers were flying everywhere. He jumped out of bed and pinned me on my back.

"Say 'I snore.' "

"No!"

"Admit you talk in your sleep."

"No!"

He started tickling me. I giggled. "Let me up." I demanded. He kept tickling me. "I gotta pee. Let me up."

"Not until you say 'I snore.' "

"You snore." I said laughing. He tickled me more and rubbed his nose against mine; suddenly our lips connected. Morning breath and all. He laughed. "Oooooh, I'm gonna tell! You kissed me!" He sounded five years old.

I stood up on the bed with my hands on my hips. "Who are you going to tell?"

His tone changed from playful to worried. "We're just friends, right?"

"Get your rusty behind out of my bed and take your last night clothes-wearing self home. I got things to do today. I'm watching the Nebraska/University of Texas game at three o'clock with my friend Max." He smiled, seemingly relieved. We were still just friends.

On the way out the door he thumped me on the arm saying, "You're still my road dog, and you talk in your sleep."

I pushed him out the door, laughing, "Hurry up or you'll be late for the game."

And just like that I was completely clear. I thought I wanted romance, but I really just wanted closeness from someone I cared about. I had five hours until Max came back and the game started and I couldn't think of a better way to spend them than with myself.

25

Just L.I.G. (Let It Go)

My Grandma always said . . .
You won't fully understand until
you have to put your feet
underneath your own table.

My cell phone rang as I emerged from
the subway. It was Kay.

"Where are you? What's going on? What are
you doing tonight?"

"I'm a block from home. I'm planning to
chill out and regroup: Make dinner, take a bubble bath, have a glass of wine, and maybe even
read a book. I'm tapped out."

"Don't cook, we're coming over."

"We who?" As much as I love Kay, I really
wanted the time to myself.

"Who else? Olga, Max, and I. We'll bring the grub. You've got cards?"

Before I could say no, my cell phone beeped.

It was Max. "Where are you? Hurry up and get home."

"What's going on? Kay's on the other line."

"Stop gabbing with her and get home. Bye." Max hung up. I clicked back to Kay.

"That was Max. What are you guys up to?"

"Nothing." She sounded like a guilty seven-year-old who'd broken a vase and glued it back together. "Just get to your place." She hung up.

I halfway expected to see them on my steps when I got home. As I unlocked my door I was greeted with "SUR-PRISE!" and camera flashes.

Kay, Olga, and Max had decorated my apartment with Happy Birthday streamers and balloons and brought over Wing Wagon, french fries, Heinekens—and Cousin John's chocolate mousse cake.

"But you guys, it's a week before my thirtieth birthday . . ."

Before I could finish, Olga interrupted. "We're your best friends and we just wanted some quality birthday time with you apart from your big party.

"Come on, make a wish and blow out your candles before the smoke detector goes off." Max nudged me as the cake Kay was holding blazed with candles.

As I closed my eyes to make a wish I heard my grand-mother's voice say, *"just keep living."* And after a year of dat-ing I realized that I'd followed her advice without planning to. I had kept living. And I'd found out a lot about myself. My heart had been broken and it had healed. I had spent a whole year looking for someone else to come along and make me whole when I was the only one who could do it all along. My broken heart wasn't anyone else's fault—it was the end result of a series of choices I had made. In fact, I couldn't give the very things I was asking for. After all, how caring, thoughtful, kind, respectful, compassionate, patient, honest, affectionate, or supportive had I been to myself?

All this time I'd been trying to get it "right"—the right conversation, outfit, perfume, hairstyle, shoes, job. I'd been trying to do or be whatever I thought a Mr. Right wanted, but the question I hadn't been willing to ask had to do with what I wanted. And suddenly I was very clear. I wanted me, in all my glorious imperfection. Kissing frogs wouldn't turn them into princes, and quite frankly I don't think I even needed a prince. Lately, I seemed to be doing just fine on my own.

I blew out all thirty candles with one breath, recognizing my wish had already come true: I was no longer heartbroken; I was no longer angry; and I was with my three best friends on Friday night. What more could I want?

About the Author

Ritta McLaughlin is the vice president of an investment banking firm in New York City, where she lives.